GOD WITHOUT JESUS

The Making of Empty Religion

ADEDEJI DAVID ADEOYE

The Author of:

- *God's Trinity Demystified: The Veil Covering It Is Finally Removed*
- *Jesus and the Trinity: What Many Believers Don't Know*

ISBN: Softcover 978-1-63871-860-4
eBook 978-1-63871-861-1
Published by: PageTurner Press and Media LLC
Publication Date: 01/06/2022

To order copies of this book, contact:
PageTurner Press and Media
Phone: 1-888-447-9651
info@pageturner.us
www.pageturner.us
Front cover design by: Shederic Ibe Ehiabhi, Nigeria.
Back cover design by: PageTurner, Press and Media, USA.
Printed in the United States of America

ENDORSEMENT

Rev. Ayomide Abraham, District Overseer and Axis Coordinator, Foursquare Gospel Church, Sango Ota, Ogun State, Nigeria, says that this book is a powerful revelation from the Spirit of God on the subject it covers. My personal experience in the gospel adventure to date has spanned some forty-six years. Within this period, I have been able to uncover the secret behind casual and unfruitful Christianity. I describe casual and unfruitful Christianity as being simply religious. And in my view, religion is the quest of man to worship a deity, and there are many religions in the world.

Religion does not afford one a definite personal encounter with Jesus which leads to salvation. Salvation only occurs when a sinner believes in the atonement which the blood of Jesus provides. From this personal experience, I witness unto one fact about the author. He has been able to uncover the secret behind casual and unfruitful Christianity. It is that secret that leads to salvation which only Jesus, as Savior, provides. This is what it means, according to him, to "believe also in Jesus."

God without Jesus: The Making of Empty Religion provides sufficient light to remove the darkness into which religion has consigned any destiny over time. It is a spiritual menu which every mature believer cannot do without. It is not just another Christian literature but a researcher's manual.

God has used Adedeji David Adeoye to deepen spiritual understanding in this book. It is thus a book which every Christian should read and I so recommend.

Rev. Moses O. Daramola, a retired senior pastor and former lecturer of LIFE Theological Seminary in Sango Ota, Ogun State, Nigeria, says that the title of this book, *God without Jesus: The Making of Empty Religion* may be offensive to the adherents of some religious sects that deny the deity of Jesus Christ. But he affirms, without apology, that such religions are not able to take their adherents to God.

I clearly saw two things as I read from one chapter of the book to another. Number one is a startling revelation or elucidation which makes me to ask, "Have I really been reading the Bible?" I then realized that such revelation and elucidations could only have come from the bowels of Holy-Spirit-inspired focus, meditation, concentration and dedication to the Bible by Adedeji David Adeoye.

Number two is how Adeoye links every book of the Bible to the person and ministry of our Lord Jesus Christ. This trend reminds me of an illustration in a Sunday school manual which I read several years back. The story was told of a man who bought the map of America and tore it into pieces. He asked two little children to arrange the pieces to make the map of America. After many fruitless attempts, they were about giving up when one of them discovered that there was the picture of a man at the reverse side of the map and he shouted "There is a man in it." They turned over each piece and began to fix the picture of the man. Before long, they were done. They turned it and the map of America was perfectly made. Adeoye has done the same by linking every book of the Bible to the person and ministry of our Lord Jesus Christ.

Anybody who reads *God without Jesus: The Making of Empty Religion* will better understand the Bible and renew commitment to the Lord Jesus Christ.

DEDICATION

Abraham sent the eldest servant of his house, Eliezer, to his brethren in Padan Aram, on a singular assignment. It was to get a wife for his son, Isaac. He successfully carried out that important assignment. When reporting how the journey went, Eliezer credited the LORD with the success of getting a virtuous virgin, Rebekah, to become the wife of Isaac. He said, "…As for me, being on the way, the LORD led me to the house of my master's brethren" (Genesis 24:27).

John 14:1 is the common but major and apparently simple text from which this book is produced. The text says, "Let not your heart be troubled; you believe in God, believe also in Me" (NKJV). It was the first statement with which Jesus comforted His disciples when it was about time for Him to be crucified at Golgotha, the place of a skull. Crucifixion was how His blood was shed to atone for the soul of man. By it, He potentially saved mankind from the bondage of Satan, the Devil. From that point on, the requirement for whoever desires salvation from sin is to appropriate His blood to himself or herself.

Because the LORD led me, step by step through this text, like He led Eliezer, the chief servant of Abraham, to find a wife for Isaac, it resulted in the production of this book. This is why I dedicate it to Him in appreciation of His role. He deserves my total and unreserved appreciation.

Adedeji David Adeoye

ACKNOWLEDGEMENT

The Ministers and Leaders' In-Service Training of Mushin District of Foursquare Gospel Church, Lagos, came up in July 2019. My wife and I were privileged to be invited along with other ministers by the District Overseer, Rev. Emmanuel Attah, as facilitators. The chairman of the organizing committee of the program was Rev. Olufẹmi Williams.

The topic of my sermon was *The Life of a Total Spiritual Minister.* In the course of delivering the paper, I spoke briefly on the text of John 14:1. After the program, I continued to meditate and pray on the substance of the text and to also study it. My spiritual activities on this text ultimately resulted in the production of *God without Jesus: The Making of Empty Religion.* I, therefore, acknowledge the immense contributions of the duo of Reverends Emmanuel Attah and Olufemi Williams for inviting us.

Onome Osifo-Whiskey, my friend and long-time Managing Editor of TELL, a foremost news magazine in Nigeria, was the man that God used to encourage me to go on writing. He seemed to see what I did not seriously appreciate about myself. He was thus like the engine that drove me. I acknowledge him for his great contributions over the years.

I also acknowledge the physical and spiritual contributions of my wife. She provided, as usual, the peaceful and conducive atmosphere that I needed to meditate and the spiritual support through prayer.

Finally, I state with delight that the Lord had enabled me to be digging a well of "living water" in a vision since 1996. The first book with international standard it supplied is titled *God's Trinity Demystified: The Veil Covering It Is Finally Removed* (2014, 2018). As I continued to dig the well, my second book, *Jesus and the Trinity: What Many Believers Don't Know* (2019) oozed out from it. It is out of the same well that this third book, *God without Jesus: The Making of Empty Religion* (2021) also oozed out. I, therefore, acknowledge the invaluable works of the Spirit of God in the course of this spiritual progression.

Adedeji David Adeoye

CONTENTS

FOREWORD

The main text from which this book is produced is John 14:1. There are two slightly different variations or translations of the text in English. But whichever of the two variations one reads, the text is divided into three segments.

The first segment which says, "Let not your heart be troubled…" is translated the same way in all the available versions. The second segment has two slightly different translations. These different translations give rise to two different versions. One version includes the pronoun "you." It says, "…you believe in God…." The other version translates it without the second-person plural pronoun. It says, "… believe in God…." The third segment is translated in both versions similarly thus, "…believe also in me."

The dual translations of this text confirm that "…by the mouth of two or three witnesses every word may be established" (Matthew 18:16). This truth and how the author explains them, in my view, show how much effort he put into producing this work. Adeoye uses both translations to address the need to believe and worship both God and Jesus.

Religion had long been in practice. It originated with God. This was by way of God commanding human beings to obey Him. Obedience of His command leads to blessing, while disobedience leads to punishment.

The man and woman who made up the first humans, being husband and wife, must have loved each other. They must have also loved God with all their hearts. However, by biblical account, in Chapters 3 and 4 of Genesis, their love for each other and for God had become marred by disobedience of God's command. This led to their expulsion from the beautiful Garden of Eden where they were housed and daily enjoyed fellowship with God. Sin, thus, means, being cut off from God, the result of which is spiritual as well as ultimate physical death. How can the lost fellowship be restored? The correct answer to this question is at the basis of this book.

God's idea is that one must pass through Jesus, His only begotten Son, to get to Him after death. This is what being born again guarantees one. This means that religion is not so empowered to guarantee access into heaven. The author explains that everybody must go beyond being born of the flesh to being born again of the Spirit. Those who do so owe it a duty to spread the news through preaching and their lifestyle.

A story is told of Gordon Maxwell, a missionary to India. He requested a Hindu to teach him his language. He said, "No, I will not teach you my language." Maxwell said, "You don't understand me. I am only asking you to teach me your language." The man, known as Sahid, said, "No, I will not teach you. No man can live with you and not become a Christian.

Another story like this concerns one skeptic whose name is Lord Peter Borough. He spent a night with a Christian called Fenedon. In the morning, he hurried away saying, "If I spend another night with that man I shall be a Christian in spite of myself." Both stories show that we must live lives that will attract those who are holding unto religion to accept Jesus as their Savior. This is because He is the only one that was sent to provide man with salvation from sin and eternal damnation.

The author, Adeoye, that I know, is a co-traveller to the Promised Land. He is not only a student of the Bible but also a searcher and researcher of the word. He is also a teacher of the word of God. To God is the glory for the understanding which the Spirit of God has granted him and to share same with the world. He is an author that one should listen to. According to him, no one has control over the religion into which one is born. But as he affirms, everybody has the right to convert to "belief in Jesus." This is because there is no religion that can take anybody to God. It is Jesus alone that can, because He is the only way to Him.

There are a number of scriptural truths unveiled by Adeoye which could only have been by the Spirit as per Psalm 32:8. This text says, "I will instruct you and teach you in the way you should go; I will guide you with Mine eye." Some truths which he reveals could not have been by the flesh. It could only have been by the Holy Spirit that indwells a man of God.

As a practice, Adeoye gives close and adequate attention to the word. He would not even miss punctuation marks in the Bible. This tells a reader of his books that he is someone whom a serious learner should listen to by reading this book.

I sincerely recommend it to everyone who wants to know the will of God so as to make it to heaven. There are lots of lessons to learn from this invaluable resource material.

Rev. John M. Dansu,
Foursquare Church Pastor [Rtd.], and
Former Permanent Secretary,
Lagos State Government of Nigeria.

PREFACE

I started writing this book in July 2019. By that month, I had daily and briefly been praying for a little over sixteen years to understand the Bible. I started the exercise about May 2003. The desire is to achieve two objectives, to wit, to know Jesus, and to make Him more known. Therefore, I started a long time ago to ask, seek, and knock daily at the altar of God. My daily prayer point was to understand the Bible.

My reasons for desiring to know Jesus and make Him known are because of the content of John 17:3. It says, "And this is life eternal, that they may know You, the only true God, and Jesus Christ whom You have sent." God promises to give man eternal life which shall be enjoyed in a special place in the hereafter. In that place called heaven, "…There shall be no more death, nor sorrow, nor crying. There shall be no more pain, for the former things have passed away" (Revelation 21:4). This precious promise is obtainable through knowledge of God and His only begotten Son, Jesus Christ.

God's voice had not been heard and His shape seen (John 1:18; 5:37). Therefore, He cannot be put in a test tube like air so as to find out His qualities. In short, He cannot be known (Acts 17:23). Jesus once affirmed this truth to some Jews when He had a serious discussion with them. He had told them, "If anyone keeps My word he shall never taste death" (John 8:52). This set of Jews questioned Him in John 8:53 saying: "Are You greater than our father Abraham, who is dead? And the prophets are dead. Who do you make Yourself out to be?"

In the course of His affirmation of man not knowing the unseen God, He told them, "…If I honor Myself, My honor is nothing. It is My Father who honors Me, of whom you say, that He is your God. Yet you have not known Him…" (John 8:54–55). He openly told them, "You have not known Him." Jesus, on the other hand, once upon a time, was seen and so could be known, at least to some extent. Much is also written down about Him in the Scriptures to read and learn from. [Adeoye][1]

I suppose, therefore, that it is possible to understand what is written about Him, especially through illumination by the Spirit of God. This will help us to know Him and then believe in Him through whom eternal life can be acquired.

Since I embarked on this journey of understanding the Holy Bible with the aim of knowing Jesus and making Him more known, I have been able to author two books. They are *God's Trinity Demystified: The Veil Covering It Is Finally Removed* (2014 and 2018) and *Jesus and the Trinity: What Many Believers Don't Know* (2019). This book, *God without Jesus: The Making of Empty Religion* is the third one.

John 14:1 appears to be a simple text. The New King James' Version (NKJV) translates it thus, "Let not your heart be troubled; you believe in God, believe also in Me" (KJV). It was Jesus that spoke those words. He did in the course of His final conversation with His disciples. It was when His crucifixion was about four days away. I was so very familiar with this text that I could rehearse it off head. I could even convert it to a hymn. But I really never took time off to meditate on it until July 2019. The Spirit of God *directed* me to look at the text more closely than I had ever done. I obeyed Him.

I had, hitherto, always quoted it off head thus: "Let not your heart be troubled: believe in God, believe also in me." The Spirit of God, however, called my attention to my omission of the second-person plural pronoun "you" in the New King James' Version. But, in the course of my research, I found several other versions that translate it without the second-person plural pronoun "you." A number of them include *The NIV (New International Version) Study Bible* published by

---

[1] Adeoye, Adedeji David: For more of this divine truth, read *Jesus and the Trinity: What Many Believers Don't Know* [Published by Page Turner Press and Media, Chula Vista, California (2019)]

Zondervan Publishing House, Grand Rapids © 1973, 1978, 1984 *MI 49530, USA*. Another example is the version from the *Ancient Eastern Text* by George M. Lamsa's Translations. It is published by Harper & Row, Publishers, San Francisco. It was originally published by A. J. Holman Company, © 1933, 1939, 1940, 1957, 1961, 1967, and 1968. A third one is the popular *New Revised Standard Version (NRSV).*

Apart from minor differences in punctuation marks, several other versions also include the second-person plural pronoun "you." They are, *Darby Bible Translation, Berean Study Bible, Berean Literary Bible, New King James' Version, NET Bible, Jubilee Bible 2000*, and *Webster's Bible Translation.* One edition of *New International Version (NIV)* also includes that pronoun. Further comment on this difference shall be made in Chapter 5.

What you are about to read is the outcome of my step-by-step meditation on the text as I was guided by the Spirit of God. It is divided into seven parts consisting of 16 chapters. I pray that God will give the reader understanding of the content of this little book. It will enable the reader to know God and Jesus and to ultimately have eternal life.

Adedeji David Adeoye

INTRODUCTION

The Sacrifice of the Lamb of God in an Atmosphere of Religion

Sin is the fundamental problem of man. It is disobedience of the command of God who created him in His own image and likeness (Genesis 1:26–27). After forming him with the dust of the ground and breathed the breath of life into his nostrils, he became a living soul (Genesis 2:7). Before He formed man, He had earlier created angels (Psalm 8:5). One of them was an arch angel called Lucifer (Isaiah 14:12). Lucifer later rebelled against God. He thought in his heart to raise his throne above that of God. His plot led to a war in heaven. He was defeated in the first battle with the involvement of the Lamb of God. He was judged by being cast down to earth.

God did not originally form the body of man to be eternal. Its being eternal was to depend on His program of resurrection from the dead. This is why "...it is appointed for men to die once, but after this the judgment..." (Hebrews 9:27). Meanwhile, his body had to exist. Its existence had much to do with the three types of trees that He made to grow in the Garden in Eden. The first type consists of every tree that is pleasant to the sight and good for food. Being good for food implies that man is free to eat their fruit, leaf, bark, or root. Therefore, eating them was not sinful. Their effect on the body is for it to go on living in good health.

That eating them was not sinful is confirmed by Jesus. This is why He asks in Mark 7:18–19, "Do you not perceive that whatever enters a man from outside cannot defile him, because it does not enter his heart but his stomach, and is eliminated, *thus* purifying all foods?" And according to Apostle Paul, what man only needs to do is to receive them with thanksgiving (1 Timothy 4:3–4), bless them, and eat.

The second was the tree of life. It was in the midst of the Garden. Man was also free to eat it. Therefore, eating it was not also sinful. The effect of eating it on man's body is that it will live forever (Genesis 3:22). The third was the tree of the knowledge of good and evil. God commanded man not to eat of it. The penalty for disobedience was sure death. Therefore, it was obedience of the command of God about eating or not eating any of the trees that determines man's bodily living.

From the three types of trees, one truth is evident. It is that eating any of the three types of trees have either positive or negative impact on man. The impact is positive if he obeys God's command concerning which tree he eats. On the other hand, it is negative if he disobeys. The positive impact is life, while the negative is death. God admonishes everyone to obey so as to live (Deuteronomy 30:19–20).

The Scripture says, "A man can receive nothing unless it has been given to him from heaven" (John 3:27; 19:11). So, God did not allow Adam and Eve to eat of the fruit of life. This was an act of love by God. It was an act of love because if He allowed them to eat it, they would have consequently lived forever as flesh and blood. But as flesh and blood, they would not qualify to enter His Kingdom. This is because "…flesh and blood cannot enter the Kingdom of God" (1 Corinthians 15:50).

Lucifer later inhabited the serpent and used it as his mouth piece to deceive Eve, the wife of Adam. She ate the fruit of the tree of the knowledge of good and evil which God had earlier commanded Adam not to eat (Genesis 2:17). She gave the fruit to Adam with her and he, too, ate it. The couple knew they were naked as soon as they ate the forbidden fruit.

The LORD God came into the Garden as usual. He called on Adam. The couple had hidden themselves among the trees of the Garden. They had also sowed fig leaves to cover their nakedness. The LORD God asked Adam where he was. He said, "I heard Your voice in the Garden, and I was afraid because I was naked; and I hid myself"

(Genesis 3:10). The LORD God asked, "Who told you that you were naked? Have you eaten from the tree of which I commanded you that you should not eat?" Rather than confess his sin of disobedience, he passed the buck. He blamed God for giving him Eve, who gave him the forbidden fruit to eat.

The LORD God asked Eve, "What *is* this you have done?" She, too, passed the buck. She blamed the serpent for deceiving her and she ate the forbidden fruit. This was how Satan imported sin into the world of man. As an act of His mercy, God made coats of skin and clothed them. Surely this provision involved the killing of some animal whereby blood must have been shed. He drove them out of the cozy Garden. In order to make their salvation from sin possible, which again is an act of love, He prevented them from eating the fruit of life in their sinful state (Genesis 3:22–24).

The result of the couple's disobedience was sure death as God had earlier warned. They were to perish. Failure to enter the Kingdom of God is, thus, synonymous with perishing. But God did not create and form man and woman to perish. Hence, before He created man, He had carried out a sacrifice of His Lamb, which was Jesus, from the foundation of the world for man's salvation (Revelation 13:8). This sacrifice can be said to be done in an atmosphere of the ritual of religion. Two issues became paramount from that time till today. They include identifying and understanding what the duties of religion and Jesus, the Lamb of God, vis-à-vis the salvation of man, are.

Examples of Individual Sins of Man

After Adam and Eve were expelled from the Garden of Eden, Adam knew his wife, Eve. The conception of Eve resulted from the first time that Adam knew her. She gave birth to Cain and said, "I have acquired a man from the LORD." It is not recorded that Adam knew Eve again before Abel was born. This suggests that Eve did not conceive *again* (italics for emphasis) before Abel, the younger brother of Cain, was born. Therefore, Cain and Abel can be described as twin brothers.

The description of Cain and Abel as twin brothers needs to be proved. The first proof is that the verb "conceived" is not used again with respect to Eve before she gave birth to Abel. The one-time use of that verb in Genesis 4:1 thus covered the birth of both boys.

The first recorded example of sin committed by an individual was that of murder by Cain. He murdered his twin brother because his offering was rejected while Abel's was accepted by God. God sentenced him to a life of perpetual wandering on earth. Adam and Eve invariably lost both children. This leads to the second proof that Cain and Abel were, indeed, twin brothers. The Scripture says that "And Adam knew his wife *again*" (italics for emphasis) in Genesis 4:25. It was the result of Adam knowing his wife again that she conceived and gave birth to Seth. Seth replaced Abel.

Another example of an individual sin was that by Saul, the first king of Israel. He disobeyed two clear instructions of God. God rejected him and his entire lineage from continuing to be king in Israel.

The blessing of atonement could only be enjoyed through faith in what God did to address the sinful nature of man. This is because it is by faith alone that man can please God. Hebrews 11:6 says, "But without faith *it is* impossible to please *Him*: for he who comes to God must believe that He is, and that He is a rewarder of those who diligently seek Him."

Abraham, the First Prophet

God called Abram out of Ur of the Chaldees. He answered the call by leaving not knowing where he was going to. God promised to bless him and through him to bless the whole world (Genesis 12:1–3). Later He tested him.

He instructed him to go and offer his son, whom he loved, on a mountain that He would show him. Abram, who was later called Abraham, took the necessary steps to obey God. He and Isaac came close to the venue of the sacrifice on the third day. Isaac called his father and he answered him, saying, "Here I am, my son." Isaac asked him a very pertinent question: "Behold the fire and the wood: but where is the lamb for a burnt offering?" Abraham answered Isaac's question, saying, "My son, God will provide Himself a lamb for a burnt offering…" (Genesis 22:7–8 KJV).

During the early wandering of Abraham in the land, he had an encounter with Abimelech, king of Gerar. King Abimelech had taken Sarah, Abraham's wife. The encounter was like it happened to him in Egypt. But God told Abimelech in a dream, "You are but a dead man, for the woman whom you had taken; for she is a man's wife." Abimelech defended himself by claiming to have acted in the integrity of his heart. He wondered if God would slay a righteous nation since Abraham had told him that Sarah was his sister.

God answered him that it was because he acted in the integrity of his heart that He withheld him from sinning against Him. This is like what Joseph would say, several years after, to the wife of Potiphar, who wanted him to lie with her.

God ordered Abimelech to restore Sarah to her husband; for he is a prophet, and he shall pray for him (Genesis 20:7). This is the text in the Bible where the word "prophet" is first mentioned. And it is noteworthy that it is first used to describe the spiritual ministerial gift of Abraham, the father of faith.

The ministry of a prophet is to pray and prophesy. He is to reveal the mind of God to the people and to pray about it as led by the Spirit of God. And in this instance, Isaac was the person that Abraham first prophesied to. The prophecy served as the answer of Abraham to his question. It was thus the first prophecy which followed Abraham's inauguration into the office of a prophet by God. And the prophecy was about the provision of a lamb for a burnt offering.

If the word, "Himself," in the "prophecy" of Abraham to the question of Isaac is omitted, the rest of the prophecy will read thus: "My son, God will provide a lamb for a burnt offering." This response provides a good, correct, and sufficient answer to the question of Isaac. Why then did Abraham include it?

I submit that it would have been useless to have included it, but for its prophetic purpose. This prophetic purpose refers to the future physical sacrifice of Jesus. For as Abraham readily "sacrificed" Isaac, the son of his old age, whom he loved, so will God do. He will sacrifice His only begotten Son, whom He loves much more than Abraham loved Isaac. This prophetic purpose is further confirmed when one considers how the LORD God provided a ram as a substitute for Isaac.

The provision of a ram went thus: Abraham built an altar in the place God had told him of. He laid wood in order on the altar. He then bound Isaac his son and laid him on the wood. He stretched forth his hand and took the knife to slay him. And the angel of the LORD called unto him out of heaven, and said, "Abraham, Abraham:" and he said, "Here am I." The angel said, "Lay not your hand upon the lad, neither do you anything unto him: for now I know that you fear God, seeing you have not withheld your son, your only *son* from Me."

What followed was the miracle. "And Abraham lifted up his eyes, and looked, and behold behind *him* a ram caught in a ticket by his horns: and Abraham went and took the ram, and offered him up for a burnt offering instead of his son" (Genesis 22:13 KJV).

So, the inclusion of the word, "Himself," was quite significant. It was how Abraham, the father of faith, became the first patriarch to be called into the office of prophet by God. The call achieved two purposes. The first was that it confirmed that Abraham looked forward to the sacrifice of Jesus. The second is that Abraham kick-started the series of prophecies about the coming of the physical and singular sacrifice of Jesus. This view is confirmed by reference to the ram as, "Him", a masculine gender and not, "It", a neuter.

The future event it presents is that God the Father (the Godhead, Acts 17:29), who is otherwise called "The Soul of God," will provide His beloved Son, who is otherwise called "The Body of God" (the Godhead bodily, Colossians 2:8–9), as the Lamb of God for sacrifice. It is said in Ephesians 5:29 that no one ever yet hated his body. This truth gives a hint as to the love of God the Father for Jesus, who is "the Body of God." God shall give Him for the remission of the sin of mankind on mount Moriah, in Jerusalem.

I saw a WhatsApp post by an unknown author that made a lot of spiritual meaning to me. In a nutshell, it is about the ability of the blood of a lamb to neutralize the venom of a rattle snake. The serpent had "injected" the venom of sin into man in the Garden in Eden. Jesus, "the Body of God," is "the Lamb of God." Therefore, He was the One among the membership of the Trinity of God, whose precious blood will be required to neutralize the venom of sin in man. Little wonder that, as the Word of God, He was made flesh which contains blood (John 1:14). And, as the Lamb of God, He was slain in the spiritual realm from the foundation of the world (Revelation 13:8).

The word "Myself", which is first person singular pronoun, shows up in Jesus' statement in John 10:18. In that text, He said to His Jewish audience, "No man takes it (My life) from Me, but I lay it down of *Myself* (italics for emphasis). I have power to lay it down, and I have power to take it again. This command have I received from My Father." This was how Jesus confirmed that Abraham's prophecy referred to Him. That statement which Jesus made shows that Isaac did not struggle with his father in the course of the sacrifice. Just as Jesus obeyed the command of the Father to lay down His life, so Isaac did.

In the prophecy of Abraham to Isaac in Genesis 22:8, the name "God" thus refers to "Himself". By Jesus claiming to be the Person referred to by Abraham as "Himself", he, thus, undoubtedly, introduced Jesus in the Old Testament, His pre-incarnate era, as "God," and as well as the sent Savior. This way, Jesus introduced Himself to His audience as the God of Abraham their father. A detailed scriptural proof that Jesus is God will be presented in Chapter 9.

On account of the burnt offering by Abraham on Mount Moriah, it is confirmed that all such Old Testament offerings, beginning with Abel's, whose person and offering God had respect unto, looked forward to the sacrifice of Jesus. All such persons were adjudged to have looked forward to the sacrifice of Jesus.

And on account of the practical sacrifice of Jesus at Golgotha, those who lived or are still living in the New Testament era could look backward to it. Whoever does, automatically qualifies to enter the Kingdom of God like Abraham, the father of faith, did.

King Pharaoh that perished in the Red Sea must have read the record about the famine that ravaged Egypt and the neighboring nations. He must have also read about the role that One LORD played through someone called Joseph, a Hebrew. But at the time he was asked by Moses to recognize that LORD, he declared, "I do not know the LORD" (Exodus 5:2). This way, he chose not to look forward to Jesus, the Lord. Any person like that has only one sure destination after death. It is perdition or hell, his religion notwithstanding.

Nobody should die without taking this very vital step. This is because there is no repentance after death. Those who are looking to His sacrifice at Golgotha have the opportunity to be saved. Religion cannot save. It is Jesus that saves to the uttermost (Hebrews 7:25). But religion has its usefulness as shall also be seen.

PART I

God Is Not Partial

This part consists of three chapters. They show, by God's acts and utterances, that He is not partial.

CHAPTER 1

God Confirms His Impartiality with Birth

Conception and Birth

The *Oxford Minireference Dictionary* defines the adjective "partial" as "favoring one side or person, biased...." I would add that in some cases, this definition can be extended to include giving somebody something that such a person does not value or deserve. God does one practical thing to confirm that He is not partial. He makes the thing to apply equally to everybody in the world. It is birth.

God created man in the beginning in His image. He created them as male and female. By the breath which God breathed into the nostrils of the man that He formed with the dust of the ground, he became a living soul.

He later divided the man into male and female, each as living soul. Since then, He had been bringing people into the world, either as males or females, by one method which involves conception and birth. So, whether it concerns a black or white person, God remains committed to the same method. This is through a man and a woman mating. The woman releases a mature egg by the ovary into her fallopian tube. The man, during mating, releases semen into the woman's uterus. The semen consists of sperm and seminal fluid from the prostate gland. The semen fertilizes the egg (ovum) in the fallopian tube. The fertilized egg travels down into the uterus and is then planted in its wall. All things being equal, in nine months, a fetus, either male or female, is born.

Even with the modern complex method called *In Vitro Fertilization (IVF)*, both the egg of a woman and the sperm or seed of a man are involved.[2] A mature egg is collected from a donor. It is fertilized in

[2] https://googleweblight.com

the laboratory with sperm or seed from the man. The fertilized egg is planted in the uterus of the woman. A successful process equally results in the production of a fetus.

God also continues to give children to parents in every social setting. He does not consider differences in culture which consist of religion, color, language, geographical location, etc.

This common practice of God regarding conception and birth underlines the question that Mary asked the angel that paid her a surprise visit. Angel Gabriel had been sent to announce to her what can be termed as a very strange item of news. The angel came unto her and said, "Hail, you that are highly favored, the Lord is with you: blessed are you among women." Naturally, she was unsettled at the saying of the angel and wondered what manner of greeting she was receiving.

The angel tried to allay her fear. In doing so, he further confirmed that she had found favor with God. He then disclosed the details of the favor. It is an eight-part favor. One, she shall conceive in her womb. Two, she shall bring forth a Son. [It is not every woman who conceives that brings forth a living child. It could be still birth.] Three, she shall call his name JESUS. Four, the Son shall be great. Five, He shall be called the Son of the Highest. Six, the Lord God shall give unto Him the throne of His father, David. Seven, He shall reign over the house of Jacob forever; and eight, of His kingdom there shall be no end!

Because of Mary's prior knowledge of the method of conception and birth, she could not help asking how this shall be, seeing she knew not a man. The angel addressed her concern thus: "The Holy Spirit will come upon you, and the power of the Highest will overshadow you; therefore, also, that Holy One who is to be born will be called the Son of God" (Luke 1:35).

Mary replied by faith to the very strange information which was communicated to her by Angel Gabriel. She said, "Behold the maidservant of the LORD! Let it be to me according to your word" (Luke 1:38). Her belief in God was demonstrated in those fifteen words. At that instant, she received a supernatural visitation of the Spirit and the power of the Highest. God, thus, supernaturally sowed His Word, which is the seed of God, in her womb. They became a special fetus (flesh) in her womb, Jesus, the Son of God.

John 1:14 says, "And the Word became flesh, and dwelt among us, and we beheld His glory, the glory as of the only begotten of the Father, full of grace and truth." The Word that was made flesh consists of those thirty-three words of God which the angel communicated to her and which she believed.

This Mary, who became the mother of Jesus, was espoused to Joseph, a scion of King David. Before they were formally wedded, as per the narrative above, she was found with a child of the Holy Spirit. Because Joseph was a just man, he did not want to bring her to public ridicule. He, therefore, conceived a plan to put her away privately. While he was thinking about this, he received an unexpected visitor in a dream. So, while the visitation of Mary was physical, that of Joseph was in a dream. It was the same angel Gabriel that had visited Mary that appeared to him in the dream.

The message that the angel brought says, "Joseph, son of David, do not be afraid to take to you Mary your wife, for that which is conceived in her is of the Holy Spirit. And she shall bring forth a Son, and you shall call His name JESUS: for He will save 'His people' from their sins" (Matthew 1:20–21).

By this statement, God had literally joined them in holy wedlock. Therefore, Joseph believed the very strange message and obeyed. Jesus was eventually born. This is not news any longer. It is a known historical and unique event.

Who were the people of JESUS that He came to save from their sins? Psalm 136:3, 16 identifies who they were. The text in the KJV says, "Oh, give thanks to the Lord of lords: for His mercy endureth forever. To Him which led His people through the wilderness: for His mercy endureth forever:"

The people that the Lord led through the wilderness on their way from Egypt were the Israelites. They were the same people of the Lord whom JESUS came to save from their sins. JESUS was thus the One referred to as the Lord of lords who led the Israelites through the wilderness.

> Despite Judaism and its practices, it was still necessary for Him, the Son of God, to come physically and save them from their sins. This means that Judaism, the Jewish religion, could not save them. Only Jesus could save whoever of them would believe Him as they believed God.

What, essentially, was Israel as a nation known for? Paul, the apostle, provides the answer to this question in Romans 9:4–5. They were known for adoption, for glory, for the covenants, for the giving of the Law, for the service of God, and the promises; whose are the fathers, and of whom as concerning the flesh Christ came. What these credentials point to is that it was Jesus who established Judaism, the religion of the Jews, with its attendant practices.

Despite Judaism and its practices, it was still necessary for Jesus, the Son of God, to come physically and save them from their sins. This means that Judaism, the Jewish religion, could not save them. Only Jesus could save whoever of them would believe in Him as they believed in God. So, by God employing an unusual process to bring Jesus into the world, He had set Him apart from everybody that He had allowed and would ever allow to be born.

It Is God that Gives Children

There is no gainsaying the truth that it is God that gives children to people. The parts played by the two mates are very minimal. The experience of Jacob with his real sweet heart, Rachel, confirms this point (Genesis 30). When Rachel saw that she bore no children, she first confronted her husband, Jacob. She told him, "Give me children, or else I die." Jacob answered her intelligibly, saying, "Am I in God's stead, who has withheld from you the fruit of the womb?" Jacob was literally asking, "What part was I supposed to play that I had not carried out?" He seemed to know that, "A man can receive nothing unless it has been given to him from heaven" (John 3:27).

Rachel became wiser and then turned over to God in prayer. The result was that God remembered her. She conceived and gave birth to Joseph. She again gave birth to Benjamin. God even gave children to Cain, the man who murdered his twin brother, and whom He cursed and also declared a fugitive and a vagabond. Cain's children were so many that he was able to build a city with them and called it after the name of his first son, Enoch (Genesis 4:17).

Everyone Is Born a Sinner

Through the disobedience of Adam and Eve, the first human beings that God made in the beginning, sin entered into the kingdom of man. Everyone from that time is thus being brought forth in iniquity from his or her mother's womb. This is what it means to be born a sinner. Everyone thus falls short of the glory of God (Psalm 51:5; Romans 3:23). And it does not matter into which social setting one is born. It is because of the reality of everyone falling short of the glory of God that the message of salvation must be preached to all. And whoever believes it will be saved.

CHAPTER 2

God Is No Respecter of Persons

The Priests of Israel

God is, indeed, not partial. He cannot tolerate it. Four passages of Scripture testify to the truth that God is not partial. The first passage is with reference to the priests of Israel in the days of Prophet Malachi. Because the priests had departed from the way of God, they had caused many to stumble in the Law and have thus corrupted the covenant of Levi.

What does the covenant of Levi mean? Moses had gone up to Mount Sinai to receive the tables of the Ten Commandments. He remained with the LORD God, on the mount, for forty days. In the estimation of Aaron and the other elders, Moses was no more coming back. Aaron, therefore, fashioned a golden calf for them to worship in the wilderness. As recorded in Exodus 32:4, they said, "This *is* your god, O Israel, that brought you out of the land of Egypt!" They worshipped it with eating and dancing. This was an abominable act.

God saw what they did while Moses was away and was highly disappointed by their action. Moses, without seeing what they did, instantly interceded for them right there on the mountain. But God immediately sent him down from there to see what his people had done. They had gone back to Egypt in their heart. This was the house of bondage in which they dwelt for a little over four centuries. From it they were delivered by the mighty hand of the living God. But they, surprisingly, gave the praise for their deliverance to an idol. In Exodus 32:8, the LORD told Moses, right there on the Mount, the exact words which Aaron had told the people in Exodus 32:4. The words are "This *is* your god, O Israel, that brought you out of the land of Egypt!"

Moses came down as he was instructed by God. On seeing the calf idol which they had carved and had addressed as stated above, he reacted in a punitive manner. He called for those who were still on the LORD's side to come over to him. Only the tribe of Levi, the third son of Jacob through Leah, did. He then announced the judgment for their sinful act. He instructed the children of Levi to draw their swords. They were to move from gate to gate. In the course of their movement, they were to slay every man his brother, companion, and neighbor. The punishment for sin instantly left 3,000 people dead (Exodus 32:26–28).

The last straw that broke the resistance of Pharaoh against setting the Israelites free from his bondage in Egypt had been by the Passover event. The event left the firstborn male child of every family and of the livestock of Egypt dead. The angel of destruction passed over the houses of the Israelites and their firstborn of men and livestock were spared. God, thereafter, declared that the firstborn of the Israelites belonged to Him. They were declared as holy unto Him.

Later, in the wilderness, the census of the tribes of Israel was carried out. The result showed that the population of the tribe of Levi was 22,000 while that of the firstborn was 22,273. Because there was no substantial difference in the numbers of the two groups, thus, rather than hold unto the first born, God replaced them with the entire tribe of Levi. The excess of 273 of the firstborn over the number of the Levites were to be redeemed with five shekels per person. The total sum of 1,365 (273x5) shekels was given to Aaron the leader of the Levites and his sons (Numbers 3:39–51). This was how God compensated the tribe of Levi for choosing to be on His side. They became the priests and Levites who ministered in the sanctuary. This was the covenant of Levi.

But by the time Eli became priest in Shiloh, ministering by the priests and Levites had been abused with sin. God then sent a serious message to Eli through another minister, saying, "…I said indeed *that* your house and the house of your father would walk before Me forever. But now the LORD says: 'Far be it from Me; for those who honor Me I will honor, and those who despise Me shall be lightly esteemed. Behold, the days are coming that I will cut off your arm and the arm of your father's house, so that there will not be an old man in your house'" (1 Samuel 2:30–31).

By the time of Prophet Malachi, things have gone very awry, so very bad that God declared, "Therefore I also have made you contemptible and base before all the people, because you have not kept My ways but have shown partiality in the law (Malachi 2:9). The truth is that God would not have punished the priests for their being partial if He, too, had been partial. Whoever punishes someone else for an offense that he is guilty of is ungodly, immoral, and corrupt. These are not the attributes of God.

Handling the Issue of Rebuke in the Church

The second passage is about the shepherd. The shepherd is like the pastor of a local church. One of his duties is handling the issue of rebuke in the church of God. In the course of carrying out this important assignment, he must not be partial, especially with respect to sin. The shepherd is not to rebuke an elder publicly. But if an issue over which a member shall be rebuked concerns sin, the shepherd must not respect his or her age. He is at liberty to rebuke publicly, even an elder, so that others may fear.

Paul then charged Timothy before God, the Lord Jesus, and the elect angels, that he should observe the things without preferring one to another, doing nothing by partiality (1 Timothy 5:20–21). God, the Lord Jesus Christ, and the elect angels are called upon to witness to this pattern of behavior because they, too, would not practise partiality. Partiality is not the character of any one of them.

God Frowns at Giving Preferential Treatment

The third passage, James 2:1–5, concerns how we treat people that come into the assembly of the brethren. God frowns at giving preferential treatment to the one who comes in wearing a gorgeous dress while treating the one who comes in wearing a poor dress with disrespect. God regards such a practice as being partial.

The crux of the matter with regard to this kind of practice is about faith. The person who comes in wearing a gorgeous dress may be lacking in faith. The person, on the other hand, who comes in wearing a poor dress, may be rich in it. And faith is absolutely necessary to please God. Hence, Hebrews 11:6 says, "But without faith *it is* impossible to please *Him,* for he who comes to God must believe that He is, and *that* He is a rewarder of them who diligently seek Him." This Scripture confirms that coming into the assembly is synonymous with coming to God.

And it is the heart of the person that is coming to God that He focuses on and not necessarily his outward appearance. But because of a mere outward dress, the shepherd may be driving away the person that could have caused God to be present in such an assembly. Therefore, it becomes offensive to God for a shepherd to treat someone having spiritual right-standing with disrespect because of ordinary clothes.

Can God, however, not be regarded as being partial in favor of the poorly dressed people as against the richly dressed? The point here is that God expects that due respect be accorded everybody. Due respect must be freely given to everybody, differences in mode of dressing notwithstanding. The gorgeously dressed person should not be told to sit in a good place while telling the poorly dressed to stand somewhere or sit under someone else's foot. God thus frowns against partiality.

"...God Is No Respecter of Persons"

The fourth passage concerns the fruit of the Spirit of God. The fruit includes love, joy, peace, longsuffering, kindness, goodness, faithfulness, gentleness, and self-control (Galatians 5:22–23). The list does not include partiality and hypocrisy (James 3:17). God does not possess any iota of evil. Partiality and hypocrisy are works of the flesh, but God is a Spirit (John 4:24).

In concluding this chapter, I hereby present a testimony by Apostle Peter. It confirms that God is not partial. This testimony is in respect of Cornelius, a centurion of the band called the Italian band. He had been very religious. He and his entire household feared God. He gave much alms to the poor. He prayed to God always and also fasted. How do we define these activities other than religious? Cornelius was a classic example of a religious person. He believed in God, hence he engaged in all these activities. The religious activities of Cornelius, however, only served to recommend him for help. The help he needed was to be made known to him, his religious practices notwithstanding, for they cannot save.

God obliged him a vision. He called the angel he saw in the vision, "Lord." This was a further proof that he believed in God. In the vision, he was instructed to send for Apostle Peter. He was given the detailed description of where to find him. When Peter comes, he would tell him what he ought to do. This is like telling Cornelius, "Good as the activities you engage in are, they cannot take you to God whom you believe in. Peter will tell you how to get to Him."

Peter came as requested by Cornelius even though he was initially reluctant. He preached Jesus to him and his entire household and He baptized them with the Holy Spirit. They spoke with other tongues like the disciples did on the Day of Pentecost.

The baptism with the Holy Spirit was all that Peter needed to be finally convinced that God is not partial. He then declared, "In truth I perceive that God shows no partiality. But in every nation whoever fears Him and works righteousness is accepted by Him" (Acts 10:34–35). So, indeed, God is not partial. And the way He earlier handled the non-readiness of Peter to go to Cornelius, showed that He condemns partiality.

A time came for the leadership of the Church to decide whether or not to accept other nations into membership of the Church. The testimony of the experience of Peter with Cornelius was all that Peter needed to convince the Council of Elders. Peter rose up in the meeting and said unto them: "Men and brethren, you know that a good while ago God chose among us, that by my mouth the Gentiles should hear the word of the gospel and believe. So God, who knows the heart, acknowledged them by giving them the Holy Spirit, just as *He did* to us, and made no distinction between us and them, purifying their hearts by faith. Now therefore, why do you test God by putting a yoke on the neck of the disciples which neither our fathers nor we were able to bear? But we believe that through the grace of the LORD Jesus Christ we shall be saved in the same manner as they" (Acts 15:7–11).

This way, God convinced the leadership of the early Church and the world at large, that He is not partial.

CHAPTER 3

"Jacob Have I Loved, but Esau Have I Hated"

The Scripture says, "…Jacob have I loved, but Esau have I hated…" (Romans 9:13–16). This Scripture tends to present God as partial. This is much more so because God hated him even before he was born! This statement is further compounded, apparently, by the fact that He will have mercy on whom He will have mercy, and compassion on whom He will have compassion. And as concluded by Apostle Paul, "So then *it is* not of him that wills, nor of him that runs, but of God that shows mercy."

All of mankind, as seed, were in the loins of Adam and so sinned in him because of his disobedience of the command of God.

God's statement about Esau, understandably, shows that He knew everything about him even before he was born. He is Omniscient; therefore, He also knows everything about everybody.

The Scripture says, "For all have sinned, and come short of the glory of God" (Romans 3:23 KJV). All of mankind, as seed, were in the loins of Adam and so sinned in him because of his disobedience of the command of God. Therefore, even before Cain and Abel were born, they had sinned in their father. It is called inherited sin to which personal sins would naturally be added. But whom will God have mercy on? It is he that repents of his or her sins against God and forgives others their trespasses. He would not bend the rules to favor anyone. He is righteous in His dealings with mankind.

Instead of repenting, Adam blamed God for giving him the woman that gave him the forbidden fruit to eat through which he sinned. From Adam's response to the charge of disobedience, it, somehow, became a condition for man to desire a thing before God would give anything.

What a man does not desire, if it is given to him, he may not value it. He may even despise it.

Esau actually despised his birthright which should have qualified him for double inheritance as the first son. He despised it by selling it to Jacob for a pottage of lentiles and a piece of bread. His case thus reinforces the need for man to desire a thing before God would give it to him. In the alternative, Jacob desired to be 'Number One.' Perhaps that was why he held the heel of Esau, though unconsciously, at their birth. He, consequently, somehow, got the birthright by purchase.

Reuben, the first son of Jacob had sexual affair with Bilhah, the third wife of his father. That was a sin for which his father cursed him (Genesis 49:3–4). Because of this sinful sexual act, Jacob, Reuben's father, punished him by transferring the birthright to Joseph, the eleventh son (1 Chronicles 5:1). Esau's sale of his birthright, because of hunger, was also punishable by God, the overall Father.

Jacob repented of his life of scheming. This he did in the course of his fight with a man on his way back from Haran to Canaan. He called the name of the place Peniel: for I have seen God face to face, and my life is preserved (Genesis 32:24–30).

He had earlier sent a drove of animals with his servants ahead. They were intended as gifts to Esau. These were meant to appease him for swindling him. Jacob was afraid to meet Esau when he was able-bodied, how much less now that he limped and Esau approached him with 400 able-bodied men! He, however, still attempted to scheme his way out of this challenge by arranging the mothers and their children in a special formation. He put Pilhah and Bilhah and their children in front. He followed them with Leah and her children. At the back were Rachel and Joseph. This arrangement was, perhaps, intended to minimize his loss should Esau decide to attack from the front. He did not know that God had taken control over any ugly situation from happening.

He then went forward, ahead of the three groups, so as to be the first to meet his brother, Esau. Jacob bowed to the ground seven times, until he came to Esau. After the seventh time, it was Esau that ran forward, embraced him, and fell on his neck, kissed him, and they wept. God had intervened to bring about reconciliation.

It was time to introduce each woman and her children at the instance of Esau. "Who are these with you?" Esau asked. This was when Jacob called himself Esau's servant. Group by group, the women and their children came forward to be introduced to him. They ended each introduction with a bow to Esau.

Esau next turned to ask what the drove of animals which he met earlier meant. This was when Jacob addressed Esau as his "lord." He said, "*These are* to find favor in the sight of my 'lord'" (Genesis 33:8). Esau acknowledged the blessing of God by declaring that he had enough. But Jacob insisted he took the presents in appreciation of the favor he had received from him. Seeing the face of Esau, for him was like he had seen the face of God! Jacob successfully persuaded Esau and he took the presents (Genesis 33:11).

There is an adage among the Yoruba in Nigeria. It goes thus, "If you see a family in which peace reigns, it is because the bastard in it has not grown up." Esau had been pacified by the gestures of Jacob. But his descendants through the Amalekites, as the arrowhead, eventually took up arms to revenge the past act of Jacob.

This was how it happened. One of the wives of Esau, Adah, gave birth to Eliphaz. God blessed Eliphaz with children. He, however, decided to add Timna, as a concubine. It was Timna that gave birth to Amalek (Genesis 36:4, 10–12). The lineage of Amalek, who was like "a bastard," became the die-hard adversary of the descendants of Israel. Hundreds of years later, his lineage, known as the Amalekites, came from behind to attack the Israelites in the wilderness on their way from Egypt.

The attack was meant to revenge the agelong issue between their fore-fathers, Esau and Jacob. God gave Israel victory over the Amalekites in this first encounter through their spiritual and physical encounters. Moses fought the spiritual battle on the mountain with his rod raised and his hand supported by Aaron and Hor. Joshua and the soldiers on the field fought the physical battle in the valley below. Because of what the Amalekites did, God promised to engage in war with that lineage forever (Exodus 17:8–16). Indeed, whoever fails to forgive others their sins should not hope to enter into the kingdom of God (Matthew 18:21–35).

Though the Amalekites were defeated in this first encounter, they didn't give up their antagonism. Soon after, Edom, the name for the entire lineage of Esau, which included the Amalekites, did not allow the Israelites to pass through their highway. They came armed to stop them passing along their border (Number 20:14–21). The Israelites had to turn away from continuing their journey along the border of Edom. They also later rejoiced over the destruction brought upon the descendants of Jacob by some external forces (Amos 1:11–12; Obadiah 1:6-15).

The role that Amalek played could be likened to that of Abimelech, the son of Gideon. Like Amalek, he was also born to Gideon by his concubine. Abimelech conspired with the men of Shechem, the people of his mother, to kill all the seventy children of Gideon. He carried out such atrocity so as to take over leadership of Israel after his father Gideon. But he did not live to actualize his dream. He was killed by a millstone which a woman threw at his skull (Judges 9:53–55).

God watches over every evil that anybody does. He will at His own time repay the wickedness of the wicked who fails to forgive others their sins. He will also reward the righteousness of the righteous.

Esau Found No Place of Repentance

Worse still, there is no record that Esau repented of his sin before God. The Scripture says that afterward, when he would have inherited the blessing, he was rejected: for he found no place of repentance. The place of repentance that Esau did not find must have been like "Jacob's Peniel." As earlier noted, it was at Peniel that Jacob settled his score with God (Genesis 32:24–30) and was ultimately blessed. And so, though, Esau sought the blessing carefully with tears, yet he lost it forever (Hebrew 12:16–17).

Esau Took a Wrong Step

The above-stated points notwithstanding, Esau compounded his lot through a wrong step with regard to a law of God. This law of God says that all that open the matrix, that is the first birth of man, and every firstling that comes of a beast belongs to the LORD (Exodus 13:12). The first birth of man that belongs to God would naturally enjoy exceptional provision and protection of the Owner, God. As for male beasts, the firstling, such as cows, sheep, and goats, which are clean, belong to the LORD. If the beast, however, is an ass, the owner would redeem it with a lamb. That the ass is redeemed makes it a safe means of transport for any rider. The owner would also adequately provide its need. But if the owner would not redeem it with a lamb, the law of God requires that he breaks its neck (Exodus 13:12–13).

Particularly as it concerns a man and a beast, as per the instruction of God concerning non-redemption of an ass, the future of anything or anybody that is not redeemed is doomed. This is a curse. It does not matter, therefore, if the owner of the ass breaks its neck at its birth or not. Since it will, ultimately, be a dangerous means of transport, it is better dead early than cause a man's death later before it is killed. Resources need not be wasted to feed it to old age only for it to become unsafe for human use. More importantly, the ass had a role to play in the course of the earthly ministry of Jesus.

God knew that Esau would be born before Jacob. By being born first, he would have the privilege of a double portion of inheritance (Genesis 48:5; 1 Chronicles 5:1; Ezekiel 47:13). But after birth and having come of age, surprisingly, he sold the birthright to Jacob for a mess of pottage of lentiles and a piece of bread. He showed that he did not desire the blessing of the birthright, and most importantly, the blessing of Abraham. This strange transaction between them had two serious implications for Esau. The first is that he chose to snub God over His ownership of him. It was like saying, "I don't need God," and "I will not serve Him either." The second is that, by the unusual sale, he also chose to be irredeemable.

The hidden implications of "both decisions" are also two-fold. Jesus said, "Do not call anyone on earth your father; for One is your Father, He who is in heaven" (Matthew 23:9). The first follow-up hidden implication of Esau's action was that he had rejected to have God be his Father. As if that was not bad enough, there was the second and hidden, follow-up implication. It concerns Jesus as the Redeemer or Savior of man from sin. Therefore, the second hidden implication of the decision of Esau was that he had also rejected his redemption by the Son of God. And whoever is not redeemed by the blood of Jesus is eternally doomed. So, God could not love him. This was much more so because he first chose to hate Him! Whoever rejects God should not expect God to love him or her (Exodus 20:5–6).

Esau Was the Odd Man Out

As noted in the *introduction,* Abraham looked forward to the sacrifice of Jesus by prophesying about it (Genesis 22:8). Isaac, in his own case, became a type of Jesus. His father that loved him "offered" him on Mount Moriah (Hebrews 11:17–19) in obedience to God's instruction. The offering of Isaac by Abraham was a type of the offering of Jesus by God. He offered His beloved Son, in whom He is well pleased, for the sin of the world at Golgotha. Jacob, like Abraham, his grandfather, also looked forward to Jesus and prophesied exhaustively about Him. This was especially with respect to his prophecy over Judah (Genesis 49:8–12). He described Jesus in it as the Shiloh that was to come, and unto whom the gathering of the people shall be. The lineage of Judah became the tribe through which Jesus came to the world. The name of the religion of the Jews, Judaism, is derived from his name.

Esau was thus the odd man out of this household of faith. I imagine that his example could be a reason for the Scripture saying, "...without faith *it is* impossible to please *Him*" (Hebrews 11:6). Esau did not look forward at all to the Redeemer of mankind.

The lineage of Judah became the tribe through which Jesus came to the world. The name of the religion of the Jews, Judaism, is derived from his name.

Isaac, his father, wanted Esau, who was the first son, to belong to God, and to be useful to Him. He took a step in that direction by asking him to go out to the field, and bring him *some* venison and make him savory meat, such as he loved. Esau was to bring it to him. He would then eat, that his soul might bless him before he died. But by being the odd man out through the wrong step that he had earlier taken to sell his birthright, he had scripturally and spiritually disqualified himself. He lost the birthright and the blessing to Jacob. Weeping later could not restore it to him.

A Vital Lesson to Share

I shall conclude this narrative about Esau with a very vital lesson to teach. Actually, Jacob did not need to be involved in the scheming that he was into. The experience of Joseph which was caused by the hatred of his siblings, confirms this lesson. His siblings sold him into slavery. Their action was intended to abort the fulfillment of the dream of greatness he had and which he narrated to them. An officer of Pharaoh,

Potiphar, in Egypt, bought him from those who had earlier bought him from his siblings. Potiphar's wife told a lie against him. She alleged that he attempted to lie with her, even though she was the one who tempted him to lie with her.

Behind the scene, however, was Satan, who was scheming to abort God's plan regarding the nation of Israel. The young man repeatedly rejected her sinful offer. He regarded it as wickedness and sin against God. She then reported Joseph to her husband accusing him of an attempt to rape her. The husband believed her report and consequently sent him to prison. Joseph interpreted the dreams of the butler and baker of Pharaoh who were also cast into the same prison. Pharaoh, eventually, had a dream but there was nobody to interpret it. This was when the butler remembered Joseph. He then recommended him by citing his dream to which he gave a profound, correct interpretation in prison. He was brought before Pharaoh and he successfully interpreted the dream. In order to carry out his recommendations so as to mitigate the effect of the impending famine, Joseph was appointed by Pharaoh as Prime Minister. His dream of greatness was finally fulfilled.

Has the LORD God given you a vision of greatness? Do not try to help yourself through human scheming. Just ensure that God is with you. As you do, the LORD God who gave the vision will work things out at His appointed time. Joseph took every event as it came. He was, however, ensuring that God was with him by not committing sin. But, Jacob, who was encouraged by the mother, tried to help himself. He got engaged in dubious practices for the vision to be fulfilled. Behind the scene, of course, was also Satan, the Devil, who was manipulating the members of this family.

"What Is Your Name?"

Jacob had great grace to enable him engage in the serious fight at Peniel. He fought to a standstill, but with no victor or vanquished. And because the Man needed to go away before day break, he urged

Jacob to let Him go. Jacob, however, would not let Him go without obtaining a blessing from Him. This was when the Man asked him a most important question: "What is your name?"

He answered the question correctly: "Jacob." This way, he acknowledged his dubious past during which he, with subtlety, supplanted Esau. He did not try to cover his past track record of unrighteous dealings. He had genuinely repented. At this crucial point, the Man gave him a new name: "Israel," which means "Prince." This was the embodiment of the blessing of Abraham which his father, Isaac, had prophesied on him. Dear reader let God take over your battle. He is able, and abundantly so.

Four Lessons to Learn

There are four lessons to learn about God's hatred for Esau as against love for Jacob. The first is that either of the two attitudes of God, as in this case, can be anybody's lot. The second is not to judge God by regarding Him as partial. This is because God knows anyone more than anyone knows oneself. The third is to diligently seek the will of God and endeavor, by all means, to do it. The fourth is that whoever would neglect God's will and yet expect Him to love him or her is deceiving himself or herself. In the same vein, whoever would respect the will of God and strive to do it, God will love him or her. What a man or woman sows, that shall he or she reap. It is foolishness to deceive oneself.

PART II

The First Segment of John 14:1: "Let not Your Heart Be Troubled..."

This part consists of one chapter. It addresses the imminent death by crucifixion of Jesus. His crucifixion will certainly cause the hearts of the disciples to be troubled. Therefore, it addresses how to scripturally handle any form of trouble that a man may have.

CHAPTER 4

"Let Not Your Heart Be Troubled…"

The Ancient of Days

The words of wise and aged people are noteworthy. They are especially so when they come close to their time to pass away. The note-worthiness of the final words of such people applied to Jesus. This is more so as He is the wisdom of God (1 Corinthians 1:30) to whom the phrase, "the Ancient of Days," applies. This is despite the few years He spent on earth as the Son of God.

Daniel 7:9 says, "I watched till thrones were put in place, and the Ancient of Days was seated; His garment was white as snow, and the hair of His head was like pure wool. His throne was a fiery flame, its wheels a burning fire." This was like the picture of Jesus that Apostle John beheld on the Isle of Patmos to which he was banished by the anti-Christ government of his day. John's description of Jesus goes thus: "His head and hair *were* white like wool, as white as snow; and His eyes like a flame of fire; His feet *were* like fine brass, as if refined in a furnace, and His voice as the sound of many waters" (Revelation 1:14–15).

But He had to take on flesh so that He could be liable to die. He could, therefore, have the sin of the world nailed to the cross in His flesh. Apostle Paul by the Holy Ghost says in Colossians 2:14–15, "And you, being dead in your trespasses and the uncircumcision of your flesh, He has made alive together with Him, having forgiven you all trespasses, having wiped out the handwriting of requirements that was against us, which was contrary to us. And He has taken it out of the way, having nailed it to the cross."

Jesus was to give His sinless life as a ransom for the soul of sinful man. God would take the sin of man and nail it to His body on the cross. This was how God would lay on Him the iniquity of us all, according to the prophecy of Isaiah. That prophecy says, inter alia, "All we like sheep have gone astray; we have turned, every one, to his own way; and the LORD has laid on Him the iniquity of us all" (Isaiah 53:6).

"...Death, a Necessary End"

According to the renowned William Shakespeare of English literature, "...death, a necessary end, will come when it will come."[3] And when it comes, it often leaves the relatives of the dead with sorrow. The disciples of Jesus, by His departure through crucifixion, were soon to become sorrowful. Because the words of the wise and aged people who are about to pass away are noteworthy, especially those of Jesus, the Ancient of Days, it was necessary to take heed to what He would say. It was sure to minimize the sorrow that would burden the hearts of His disciples.

Therefore, He first addressed them about how to combat the impending sorrow. He said, "Let not your heart be troubled; you believe in God, believe also in Me. In My Father's house are many mansions: if *it* were not *so,* I would have told you. I go to prepare a place for you. And if I go and prepare a place for you, I will come again, and receive you to Myself; that where I am, *there* you may be also. And where I go you know, and the way you know" (John 14:1–4). These are comforting words, indeed.

The throne of God in man is in his heart. If he allows it to be troubled, which means "to be disturbed," he may most likely lose it to fear. Fear is of Satan, the Devil. Such a man would have thus carelessly surrendered his heart to occupation by the arch enemy of God. It is not a good alternative. Hence, Jesus encouraged them to be determined not to let it be troubled. And the greatest spiritual force to help them

---

[3] Shakespeare, William: *Julius Caesar* https://www.britannica.com>topic>Julius....

to prevent it from happening is through belief in God and Himself. It is through it also that they would be able to get to God after their own physical death.

Before Jesus made the statement in John 14:1, Judas Iscariot had left the group. After announcing the certainty of His crucifixion and the forth-coming ignoble denial by Peter, He first said, "Let not your heart be troubled; you believe in God, believe also in Me." This text is divisible into three parts. It serves as an introductory statement to the deep things He would make known at that crucial fellowship with His disciples. And because the state of their individual heart can make or mar the expected reception of His statement, He addressed it to that part of them. But for someone not to let his or her heart be troubled, he or she must receive the enablement from heaven.

This fundamental truth has been confirmed by the Scripture that has earlier been referred to. For the sake of emphasis, that truth, according to John the Baptist, says, "...A man can receive nothing unless it has been given to him from heaven" (John 3:27). Jesus Christ, also, confirmed this truth. This was when Pilate asked Him where He came from during His trial. Jesus did not answer his question. Pilate then asked Him if He knew that he had power to crucify Him and had power to release Him. Jesus answered Pilate, "You could have no power at all against Me unless it had been given you from above" (John 19:11).

Jesus says in Mark 11:24, "Therefore I say unto you, what things soever you ask (desire), when you pray, believe that you receive *them,* and you shall have *them."* If Verses 25 and 26 of this Chapter of Mark are included, there are seven sequential actions to take so as to have what one asks. They include "forgive" and "repent," "ask (desire)," "pray," "believe," "receive," and "have." All of these are very important. On this occasion, of the seven sequential actions, Jesus focused on one, "believe." He identified two sources of enablement. They are God the Father and Jesus, His beloved Son.

The first source, which is God the Father, has two conditions to fulfill. The two conditions, as per this treatise, are derived from the two slightly different ways some English Versions translate this second part of the text. One version translates it thus: "You believe in God…." This translation refers to someone who already believes in God. It is by such a person's belief in God that He will enable him or her not to let his or her heart be troubled.

Another version translates it thus: "Believe in God…." The pronoun, "you," is omitted. This translation refers to someone who is commanded to believe in God. This implies that as soon as he or she obeys by believing in God, God will then give the needed enablement whereby his or her heart will not be troubled.

The second source, which is Jesus, has just one condition attached. This is because that part is translated the same way by every known version. The condition is to obey the command to "believe also in Jesus."

It needs be noted that as at this time of talking to the disciples, Jesus was still physically on the earth. He was, there, seated in the midst of the eleven disciples in one of the places He had chosen as a hiding place in the Upper Room, in Jerusalem. Despite His visible presence among them, He already indicated His ability to give them the needed enablement from heaven. Wow! This amounted to a claim by Him to have power as God.

> For, as the ground of the earth is the place in which seed is sown, so is the heart of man the part of him in which the word of God, His seed, is sown.

The Heart Is as the Ground

The heart of man can be compared with the ground. For, as the ground of the earth is the place in which a seed is sown, so is the heart of man the part of him in which the word of God, His seed, is sown.

Suppose a particular ground in which a seed is sown is being repeatedly cultivated, thereby disturbing the gradual growth of its root, what will happen to the root of the seed that is growing in it? The roots will be damaged, and chances of the seed sown being fruitful will be greatly minimized. This is the picture that the verb *troubled* paints for us to see. Therefore, because of the vital role that the heart of man plays in the fruitfulness of a man, the command of Jesus to His disciples not to let it be troubled becomes at once compelling and necessary.

The Prophecy of Caiaphas, the High Priest

Jesus was drawing multitudes of people to Himself by His miracles and teachings. These works were becoming big concerns to the Pharisees, the priests, and other Jewish leaders. The Scripture says, "And one of them, Caiaphas, being the high priest that year, said to them, 'You know nothing at all, nor do you consider that it is expedient for us that one man should die for the people, and not that the whole nation should perish'" (John 11:49–50). He then prophesied that Jesus should die for that nation and not for that nation only, but that also He should gather together in one the children of God that were scattered abroad (John 11:52).

Jesus Christ, Our Passover Lamb

The prophesied and necessary death of Jesus by crucifixion was imminent. After it, on the third day, the Ancient of Days, Jesus of Nazareth, would be resurrected. He would then return to His Father who sent Him to the world.

In Egypt, the final miracle that compelled Pharaoh to let the Israelites go away from their agelong bondage was by the means of the Passover feast. Each family was instructed to take a lamb or goat of one year old. It must be without blemish. It was taken from the herd on the tenth day of the first month *(Abib)* and kept until the fourteenth day. It was killed on the fourteenth day and its blood used to mark the lintel and door posts of each house. In that night, an angel of destruction passed by every house in Egypt. Every house where the blood was sighted, such families were spared death. In the houses of the Egyptians where such blood was not seen, their first born of man and beast were killed.

After making a final presentation of Himself as the Light to the world in John 12:36, Jesus then went into hiding (John 12:36). This was intended by Him to become our Passover Lamb (1 Corinthians 5:7). He, therefore, went into hiding without having committed any sin. By the time He came out four days later, he had become our Passover Lamb without blemish. He then qualified to be crucified for the remission of the sin of mankind. This was just as the blood of the lamb without blemish in Egypt was the means of salvation from Egyptian bondage.

Jesus Christ, the High Priest of Our Profession

The first place Jesus hid with His twelve disciples was in the house of Simon the leper in Bethany (Matthew 26:6; Mark 14:1–3; John 12:36). One Mary came in there with a bottle of alabaster oil of spikenard. She broke the bottle and poured the content on the Lord Jesus. This was how He was physically anointed for His priestly office. On one of His four days in this first hiding place, Judas Iscariot went out. He went to negotiate with the Jewish leaders on how he could hand Jesus, his Master, over to them, and at a price. After agreeing the price, he returned to the group. This, indeed, was an act of utter betrayal.

The Scripture says, "He who dwells in the secret place of the Most High shall abide under the shadow of the Almighty" (Psalm 91:1). Jesus had taken this venue as a temporary hiding place in order to fulfill the Scripture. Judas Iscariot, however, was going away from it to hold a meeting with the elders. The singular agenda of the meeting was how he might hand over his Master to them secretly, and at what price. I perceive that Satan met him unprotected and entered him hook, line, sinker and the fisherman's boot. He thus became fully ready to betray his Master.

Jesus Christ Established the New Testament

The second place where Jesus hid with the disciples was in the Upper Room in Jerusalem in the house of an unnamed host (Mark 14:15–17; Luke 22:7–14). It was there He celebrated His last Passover feast with His disciples. He also established the New Testament in His body and blood there. Who "the seed of the serpent" was, according to Genesis 3:15, was here revealed to be Judas Iscariot and Himself "the Seed of the woman." Judas Iscariot stormed out of this venue as soon as he was exposed to be the seed of the serpent (John 13:18, 21–30).

The third hiding place was in the Garden of Gethsemane (Matthew 26:36-46; Mark 14:32). This was where Jesus totally submitted to the will of the Father to drink the cup that the Father put in His hand. Peter who promised to suffer and perhaps die for Him could not even assist Him in prayer for one hour. He and the others were busy sleeping. Jesus came back from where He went to pray at the end of the third session. He summoned all the disciples, saying, "Rise, let us be going. See, My betrayer is at hand" (Luke 14:42). While He was still speaking, Judas Iscariot reappeared. He came that night with a detachment of the state security personnel to arrest Him.

The Trial of Caiaphas, the High Priest

Following the arrest of Jesus as He was emerging from His third place of hiding, the Garden of Gethsemane, He was first tried before Caiaphas. Several false witnesses came forward to testify against Him. Finally, two witnesses accused Him of claiming to be able to destroy the temple of God, and to raise it up in three days without hands (Matthew 26:61; 27:40; Mark 14:58; 15:29).

A few days earlier, some people had turned the temple into a market place. There they sold oxen, sheep, doves, and also converted it to a modern bureau de change. Jesus made a scourge of small cords and drove them out of the temple. The last two witnesses might have been among those whom He drove out of the temple. If that was the case, they probably used His statement against Him. This was despite the truth that He was only referring to Himself, for the temple refers to His body, which houses God. The three days refer to about how long He would remain in the grave before being raised up. Jesus did not defend Himself against any of the charges which the false witnesses brought against Him. Caiaphas then arose, as in a rage, and said unto Him, "Do you answer nothing? What *is it* these men testify against You?" Jesus still kept mute.

At this juncture, Caiaphas said unto Him, "I put You under oath by the living God: tell us if You are the Christ, the Son of God!" In answering his question, Jesus said, "*It is as* you said. Nevertheless, I say to you, hereafter you will see the Son of Man sitting at the right hand of the Power, and coming on the clouds of heaven" (Matthew 26:64).

The claim of Jesus to be the Son of Man opened up two key issues. Both issues are connected with Saul the first man whom God chose as King of Israel and David whom He later chose to replace him. God anointed both of them through Prophet Samuel. The first issue is about Jesus being the Son of Man and the second is about Him being the High Priest among His brethren. Both issues highlight the prime role of obedience of God's command.

The first key issue was derived from the episode of Prophet Samuel coming to offer burnt and peace offerings at Gilgal. King Saul was mandated to wait for him for seven days. After the offerings, Saul would then go up in arms against the Philistines. Because Samuel had not yet come, he first offered the burnt offering. He was to go ahead to offer the peace offering when Samuel showed up. He disobeyed the command of God which Samuel communicated to him. Samuel, immediately, declared God's punishment for his disobedient act thus,

"But now your kingdom shall not continue. The LORD has sought for Himself a man after His own heart, and the LORD has commanded him *to be* commander over His people, because you have not kept what the LORD commanded you" (1 Samuel 13:14).

The man that the LORD found in the course of His search was David. He found him in the wilderness where he was tending his father's sheep. He became the man that the LORD promised to give an everlasting kingdom and throne (2 Samuel 7:16). It was through his lineage that Jesus, the Son of God, came. This was how Jesus acquired the title, "The Son of Man."

The second key issue referred to God's command through Prophet Samuel to Saul to go and destroy the Amalekites. It would be remembered that Saul did not fully obey God's command. Prophet Samuel pronounced his rejection by God from being king over Israel any longer because of his disobedience. As Samuel turned to go, King Saul held his mantle in an attempt to compel him to go and worship God with him. Prophet Samuel's garment tore in the process. King Saul had thus uncovered Prophet Samuel. God consequently removed King Saul from the throne. He replaced him with David, the son of Jesse of the lineage of Judah. Caiaphas, the high priest, suffered the same fate as King Saul.

The answer that Jesus gave to Caiaphas' question above angered him so much that he tore his clothes. In doing so he said, "He (Jesus) has spoken blasphemy! What further need do we have of witnesses? Look, now you have heard His blasphemy!" It was unanimously declared that Jesus was guilty as charged and deserved death. But it was not Jesus that was guilty. Instead, it was Caiaphas, the high priest, who was guilty. He violated the priesthood law. He did by renting his clothes in the process of pronouncing Jesus guilty.

The law that God handed down through Moses expressly states in Leviticus 21:10, "*He who is* the high priest among his brethren, on whose head the anointing oil was poured and that is consecrated to wear the garments, shall not uncover his head, nor tear his clothes." Whoever does is automatically disqualified from continuing in that office. This was how Caiaphas physically, practically and publicly disqualified himself from continuing in the office of high priest. God also physically, practically and publicly gave the vacant office of High Priest to Jesus of the lineage of David, from the tribe of Judah. This was because He was not guilty and was indeed the Son of God and the Son of Man.

It was Caiaphas, the high priest, who was guilty. He violated the priesthood law. He did by renting his clothes in the process of pronouncing Jesus guilty.

With that office literally and summarily abolished, the physical temple had thus run its full course. It no more had *locus standi.* It had to go. Its place was taken over by the true tabernacle in heaven where the Apostle and High Priest of our profession, Jesus, had entered into.

He is ministering there as the Son of man with His precious blood which He shed for the remission of sin of man. He will also come the second time from there as per a part of His answer to Caiaphas' question. The two men who appeared after Jesus ascended to heaven confirmed Jesus' answer. They said to the disciples of Jesus at the place of His ascension: "Men of Galilee, why do you stand gazing up into heaven? This *same* Jesus, who was taken up from you into heaven, will so come in like manner as you saw Him go to heaven" (Acts 1:11). He will come as the Son of Man.

PART III

The Second Segment of John 14:1: "...You Believe in God..." Or, "...Believe in God..."

This part consists of two chapters. They shed light on what Jesus meant by the second segment of His statement in John 14:1. The text has been translated slightly differently in several English versions.

The two slightly different translations confirm the Scripture which says that in the mouth of two or three witnesses every word may be established (Matthew 18:16; John 8:17). The two translations merge on the subject of religion such as Judaism.

CHAPTER 5

Interpretation of:

"You Believe in God" and "Believe in God"

Translation of a text of Scripture from one language to another is not an easy task. As noted under *Preface* and in Chapter 4, several English versions of the Bible translate John 14:1 slightly differently. For example, the King James' Version (KJV) includes the second-person plural pronoun "you." Its translation goes thus: "Let not your heart be troubled; you believe in God, believe also in me."

In the *Preface,* I said that I had hitherto always rendered the text off head thus: "Let not your heart be troubled; believe in God, believe also in me." This was not until one day that the Spirit of God "called" my attention to my omission of the second-person plural pronoun "you" in my copy of the King James' Version. In the course of my research, I found several other versions that actually rendered it without that pronoun.

This minor difference can cause contention. The contention could center on identifying which translation of the original language of the manuscript is accurate and which is not. This likely contention needs to be properly and correctly addressed. This vital step will certainly help in correctly interpreting the text. Therefore, this minor difference is being addressed first before going on to interpret it. It is note-worthy that the third segment of the text is virtually the same in both English versions. That it is the same in both versions shows that the contention can be easily addressed.

Firstly, let us assume that the versions that translate it as, "Let not your heart be troubled; you believe in God, believe also in me" are accurate. If they are, the third segment which is "...believe also in me," when joined with the second segment which is "…you believe in God," would make a good interpretation. The good interpretation would be that Jesus acknowledged or recognized the belief of the disciples in God and would also acknowledge or recognize their belief in Him. But this would be by them acknowledging or recognizing Him to be God.

Secondly, let us assume that the versions that translate it as, "Let not your heart be troubled; believe in God, believe also in me," are also accurate. If they are, the third segment which is "…believe also in me," when joined with the second segment which is "…believe in God," would also make another good interpretation. The good interpretation would be that Jesus commanded His disciples to "believe in God." This command requires them to obey God. Jesus next requires them to "…believe also in Him" as they "…believe in God." This also is a requirement to obey His command. And a call to obey Him implies that He had hitherto commanded them. It is no wonder that before this moment, Jesus had said to His disciples, "A new commandment I give to you, that you love one another; as I have loved you, that you also love one another" (John 13:34). By the second translation, therefore, they are required to obey God and Him.

Proceeding in conformity with the first translation, if the presence of someone in a gathering is acknowledged or recognized by the master of ceremony, it is a form of honor. In this instance, Jesus was like the Master of ceremony. He honored the disciples by acknowledging or recognizing their belief in God. The honor that Jesus accorded them stemmed, first and foremost, from the honor which they accorded God by believing in Him. By going forward to command them to also acknowledge or recognize Him to be God means that He was ready to accord them double honor. The first honor comes from them acknowledging or recognizing God and the second would come from acknowledging or recognizing Him (Jesus) to be God.

Jesus likewise honored God, even as God honored Him by recognizing Him as His Son in whom He is well pleased (Matthew 3:17; 17:5). Both translations, therefore, present God and Jesus as deserving honor.

In view of the derivatives from these two slightly different translations, it is confirmed that in the mouths of two or three witnesses every word may be established (Matthew 18:16; John 8:17). The sum total of this preliminary analysis is that Jesus is God. He can, thus, mediate between God and man. No other person or religion has such influence.

If the presence of someone in a gathering is acknowledged or recognized by the master of ceremony, it is a form of honor.

It was commendable of the disciples that they believed in the God that they had not seen or known. Not everybody believes in Him. Many people do not believe that He exists. This is despite the copious records of His activities in the Bible. He demonstrated much of His activities through the Israelites in Egypt. The activities which were very miraculous led to their release from bondage in Egypt. His miraculous opening up of the Red Sea for them to pass through on dry land is note-worthy. Archaeologists, by their discovery in the Red Sea, have corroborated the record of Moses. They have confirmed that the story of the chariots, soldiers, and the Pharaoh that perished in the Red Sea is not fiction. The soldiers, headed by Pharaoh, armed to the teeth, tried to cross on the dry land which the LORD God had miraculously opened up on the Red Sea bed. They did so in pursuit of the Israelites who were ahead of them on the same route.

The Israelites successfully passed through to the other side of the shore. The rod that Moses stretched over the sea to open a way for them to pass through was again stretched over it to close it up. The waters which stood as walls on both sides of the "Red Sea Way" came back and submerged those Egyptians who were on the offensive. They sank like lead to the bottom of the sea.

Those chariots and weapons of the Egyptian army have, in our time, been discovered. It was a great feat by Professor Abdel Muhammad Gader who was associated with Cairo University's Faculty of Archaeology. They saw human bones that had become darkened by age, and hundreds of weapons and pieces of armor. They saw remains of two war chariots scattered over an area of approximately 200 square meters. Their study reveals that, "Ancient soldiers seemed to have died on dry ground since no traces of boats or ships have been found in the area"[4] The research effort which yielded this historic result took place about 1.5 kilometers into the Red Sea from the edge of the modern city of Ras Gharib.

The Bible is, indeed, a compilation of events that took place from the beginning of the world. It is dangerous not to believe in what are documented in it. Believe in them and you shall enjoy the blessings that God promises and which Jesus had confirmed.

Miracle of Unbroken Piece of Chalk

Those who do not believe that God exists are called atheists. They tend to believe that God is just a figment of the imagination of those that believe that He exists. And they are ready to ridicule those that believe that He exists. They call such people fools.

I shall briefly digress to tell the story of a professor of philosophy and his experiment with a piece of chalk. I find the story very appropriate to back up the view about the atheist. It is included with the permission of the publisher.[5]

---

[4] Google @ridnewsdailyreport.com

[5] *Our Daily Manna*, "A Daily Devotional Manual for Champions," [Pub-

The story goes thus: "There was a professor of philosophy who was a deeply committed atheist. His primary goal for one required class was to spend the entire semester proving that God couldn't exist. His students were always afraid to argue with him because of his impeccable logic. Sure, some had argued in class at times, but no one had ever really gone against him because of his reputation. At the end of every semester on the last day, he would say to his class of three hundred students, 'If there is anyone here who still believes in God, stand up!' In twenty years, no one had ever stood up. They knew what he was going to do next. He would say, 'Because anyone who believes in God is a fool. If God existed, he could stop this piece of chalk from breaking when it hits the ground. *Imagine* such a simple task to prove that He is God, and yet He can't do it!' And every year, he would drop the chalk onto the tiled floor of the classroom, and it would shatter into a hundred pieces. All of the students do nothing but stop and stare. Most of the students thought that God couldn't exist. Certainly, a number of Christians had slipped through, but for twenty years, they had been too afraid to stand up! Then a young man got admitted into the university. He was a Christian and had heard the stories about this professor. He was required to take the class for his major, and he was afraid. But for three months *of* that semester, he prayed every morning that he would have the courage to stand up no matter what the professor said or what the class thought. Nothing they said could ever shatter his faith…he hoped. Finally, the day came. The professor said, 'If there is one here who still believes in God, stand up!' The professor and the class of three hundred people looked at him, shocked, as he stood up at the back of the classroom. The professor shouted, 'You fool!!! If God existed, he would keep the piece of chalk from breaking when it hits the ground!' He proceeded to drop the chalk, but as he did, it slipped out of his fingers, off his shirt cuff, on to the pleat of his pants, down his leg and off his shoe. As it hit the ground, it simply rolled away unbroken. The professor's jaw dropped as he stared at the chalk. He looked up at

lished by Bishop (Dr.) Chris E. Kwakpovwe (CEK), Volume 19 Sections 10, 11, and 12 October – December 2019].

the young man and then ran out of the lecture hall. The young man who had stood up proceeded to walk to the front of the room and shared his faith in Jesus for the next half hour. Three hundred students stayed and listened as he told of God's love for them and of His power through Jesus."

It is, however, whoever says that there is no God that is a fool. Psalm 14:1 says, "The fool has said in his heart, 'There is no God....'" This professor used his position to distance young folks from embracing the love of God. The miracle of the unbroken piece of chalk might have eventually convinced him to believe in God. But only God can tell how many folks he had led astray into perdition over the long period of twenty years!

The Disciples Came to Jesus

The disciples came to Jesus. This was because they acknowledged or recognized Him to be the promised Messias (Messiah), which means the Christ, from the lineage of King David.

The statements of many people in the Gospels confirm this position. A prominent one among them was John the Baptist. He made some statements at the point of introducing Jesus. John says in John 1:33–34, "I did not know Him, but He (God) who sent me to baptize with water said to me, 'Upon whom you see the Spirit descending, and remaining on Him, this is He who baptizes with the Holy Spirit.' And I have seen and testified that this is the Son of God." John the Baptist also testified that "...He saw the Spirit of God descending like a dove and alighting upon Him. And suddenly a voice came from heaven, saying, 'This is My beloved Son, in whom I am well pleased'" (Matthew 3:16–17).

Before the incident reported above, the same John stood with two of his disciples. When he looked and saw Jesus walking nearby, he said to them in John 1:29, "Behold the Lamb of God who takes away the sin of the world!" The two disciples believed his testimony.

These disciples immediately left their master, John the Baptist, and followed Jesus, the Christ. One of the two disciples was Andrew. He and an unnamed disciple of John demonstrated their belief in the God that sent John the Baptist. This they did by immediately abandoning their former master and following Jesus to where He lodged. They stayed with Him overnight (John 1:39).

The following day, Andrew also immediately informed his brother Peter, saying, "We have found the Messias (Messiah)" (which is translated the Christ). Andrew brought Peter to Jesus. Peter also believed in God by becoming one of His disciples.

A very detailed testimony is that of Nathanael (Bartholomew). Philip found him and said to him, "We have found Him of whom Moses in the Law, and also the prophets wrote–Jesus of Nazareth, the son of Joseph" (John 1:45). Nathanael said to Philip, "Can anything good come out of Nazareth?" Because Philip believed that Jesus of Nazareth was the Prophet that God promised Israel through the prophecies of Moses (Deuteronomy 18:15–19) and several other prophets, he invited Nathanael to, "Come and see" (John 1:46). Nathanael agreed and followed Philip to see Jesus.

When Jesus saw Nathanael, He said to him, "Behold, an Israelite indeed, in whom is no deceit!" Nathanael could not help asking Jesus, "How do you know me?" Jesus answered him, "Before Philip called you, when you were under the fig tree, I saw you." Nathanael declared: "Rabbi, You are the Son of God! You are the King of Israel" (John 1:49). This is the core of Nathanael's belief in God who had promised to give King David an everlasting throne (2 Samuel 7:16). King David had spent considerable time before the LORD God in prayer. His sole request was that God would bring the promise He made concerning his house to come to pass. In Jesus, the promise was clearly manifesting. God is faithful.

The disciples had not seen God because He is invisible. But by believing the record and prophecies of the Old Testament about Jesus Christ, and to have willingly come to Him, He adjudged them to have believed in God.

What would I say of the vibrant historian in the person of MLM (Mister Levi Matthew)? A tax collector he was until Jesus called him at his duty post and enlisted him as one of His disciples. Matthew did not waste time to abandon his lucrative civil service employment to which great fortune with infamy was attached. He left to follow a new Master in grand style. He celebrated his departure, like Prophet Elisha of old did (1 Kings 19:21). He abandoned his infamous employment with a get-together. His former colleagues were in attendance at the party. The adversaries of Jesus, the Pharisees and the scribes, did not waste time to condemn Him. They alleged that He was eating meat with publicans and sinners. The setting, however, offered Jesus a golden opportunity to let this set of self-righteous people know that it was for such publicans and sinners that He came. He said, "Those who are well have no need of a physician, but those who are sick. I did not come to call the righteous, but sinners, to repentance" (Mark 2:17).

The disciples had not seen God because He is invisible. But by believing the record and prophecies of the Old Testament about Jesus Christ, and to have willingly come to Him, He adjudged them to have believed in God.

Matthew believed in God so much that, thereafter, he took great pains to research into the Old Testament to exhume the genealogy of Jesus. He titled its publication in Matthew 1:1 as: *The Book of the Genealogy of Jesus Christ, the Son of David, the Son of Abraham.* The collection of the material served as a vivid testimonial of his belief in

God. It was duly recognized by the Lord Jesus when He said to His disciples, "…You believe in God…."

Judas Iscariot Did not Believe in God

A vital question to find answer to is this: When did Jesus know that the disciples believed in God? The disciples, towards the end of the mission of Jesus to the world, jointly declared, "Now we are sure that You know all things, and have no need that anyone should question You…" (John 16:30). In view of the truth declared by these disciples, it is rational to believe that Jesus knew that the disciples believed in God even before He called them one after the other to follow Him.

This view can be confirmed. For example, when Andrew brought his brother Simon to Jesus, without having physically met with him before, Jesus said, "You are Simon the son of Jonah. You shall be called Cephas, which is translated, 'A Stone'" (John 1:42). Jesus did not only know his name and that of his father and that he believed in God, He also knew what his future would be like. He also told Nathanael the place where he was before Philip called him.

So, Jesus knew that Judas Iscariot did not believe in God all the while that he was following Him. He also knew that he would betray Him. The example of Judas Iscariot thus shows that everybody is called and welcomed by Jesus. Everybody is also allowed to follow Him whether he or she believes in Him and God or not. The role of Judas Iscariot, however, shall not just be glossed over. His involvement shall be given some in-depth analysis as it pertains to the issue of belief in God by the disciples.

The record of Mark says, "And He (Jesus) went up on the mountain and called to *Him* those He Himself wanted. And they came to Him. Then He appointed twelve, that they might be with Him and that He might send them out to preach, and to have power to heal sicknesses, and to cast out demons" (Mark 3:13–15). He took this action after an all-night prayer session (Luke 6:12). And Judas Iscariot became one of His twelve appointed disciples. He was even given a prominent office which required tremendous amount of trust. He occupied the office of a treasurer. He was the keeper of the purse of the group.

The involvement of Judas Iscariot goes further back in Scripture than that of every other disciple that Jesus appointed. He had a very unique scriptural role to play. While the other disciples believed in God and so were duly appointed, it was Satan, the Devil, which planted him in the company of Jesus as someone that did not believe in God. He was meant to play the role of an adversary.

The Parable of the Wheat and Tare

The role of Judas Iscariot was typified by Jesus in His Parable of the Wheat and the Tare. Jesus also "used" this parable to illustrate the Parable of the Sower.

> First of all, the Parable of the Wheat and the Tare, which is documented in Matthew 13:24–30, 37–43, shall be looked into here and interpreted.
> Another parable put He forth unto them, saying:
> "The kingdom of heaven is like a man who sowed good seed in his field:
> "But while men slept, his enemy came and sowed tares among the wheat, and went his way.
> "But when the grain had sprouted and produced a crop, then the tares also appeared.
> "So the servants of the owner came and said unto him, 'Sir, did you not sow good seed in your field? How then does it have tares?'
> "He said to them, 'An enemy has done this.' The servants said to him, 'Do you want us then to go and gather them up?'
> "But he said, 'No, lest while you gather up the tares you also uproot the wheat with them.'

> "Let both grow together until the harvest, and at the time of harvest I will say to the reapers, 'First gather together the tares and bind them in bundles to burn them, but gather the wheat into my barn.'"

The multitude, as usual, after listening to the interesting parable left the venue. They had heard but had not understood. When Jesus got back home, His disciples who were interested in understanding the parable requested Him to explain it to them. That the disciples asked for explanation is a confirmation that the multitude did not also understand the parable. Yet none of them made extra effort to seek to understand. Jesus readily interpreted the parable to the disciples.

Interpretation of the Parable of the Wheat and Tare

He answered and said unto them:

> "He who sows the good seed is the Son of Man;
> "The field is the world; the good seed are the sons of the kingdom, but the tares are the sons of the wicked one;
> "The enemy who sowed them is the devil, the harvest is the end of the world, and the reapers are the angels.
> "Therefore as the tares are gathered and burned in the fire, so it will be in the end of this age.
> "The Son of Man will send out His angels, and they will gather out of His Kingdom all things that offend, and those who practise lawlessness.
> "And will cast them into the furnace of fire. There will be wailing and gnashing of teeth.
> "Then the righteous will shine forth as sun in the kingdom of their Father. He, who has ears to hear, let him hear!"

Jesus described Himself in the parable as the sower of the good seed. And because He is one with the Father as the visible part of God, He is thus the Sower on the behalf of the Father who is invisible. So, in essence, the Father was thus the One that sowed the good seed. The good seed, otherwise called the righteous, are the ones that make up the children of the kingdom.

Jesus also described the Devil as His enemy who sowed the tares in the midst of the wheat. Of course it should be understood that the Devil was able to sow the tares because God allowed it. God once allowed him to test Job.

The good seed, otherwise called the righteous, are the ones that make up the children of the kingdom.

The tares are the ones that ended in the furnace of fire. Jesus identified the field as the world. This is to mean that Jesus was referring to human beings. They are either good or bad. The good seed are the children of the kingdom of Jesus and His Father. The tares are the children of the wicked one, whom we all know to be Satan, the Devil.

Jesus contributed His part to defeat him in heaven. This was when he attempted to dethrone God. He wanted to place himself above God. He is thus the enemy of Jesus. It is thus understandable why he came to tempt Him in the wilderness after He had fasted for forty days. He wanted to prevent Jesus from carrying out the assignment that the Father sent Him into the world for. This aim of Satan would be achieved if he could get Jesus to sin against His Father. But he woefully failed.

The harvest is the end of the world. The reapers are the angels. The plural noun, "Angels," consists of both the good and evil ones. The harvest of the wheat and tare represents the end of the world. The duty of the evil angels at the end of the world will be to gather the human beings that practised lawlessness. They shall deposit them in the furnace of fire. In that fire, they shall wail and gnash their teeth. The duty of the good angels, on the other hand, will be to gather the righteous ones that did good. They are the ones who represent the wheat. They shall be placed in the kingdom of God. They shall shine as the sun in the kingdom of God.

Application of the Parable of the Wheat and Tare

The story of Jesus and His disciples is a very good one by which we shall understand the Parable of the Wheat and Tare. It provides a practical example with which this parable can be explained and understood. This is because His disciples constituted human beings who made up a type of the two groups of the seeds sown.

Jesus, the Son of Man, who is also called the householder in this parable, sowed the good seed which represents the group of His disciples that believed in God. The Father sowed them in the kingdom of Jesus by giving them to Him (John 17:6). Satan, the Devil, who is His arch enemy, came along and sowed a bad seed, Judas Iscariot, in the midst of the eleven disciples. He represented someone in the group of Jesus' disciples that neither believed in God nor Jesus. He can be likened to witches and wizards in the present day church, who cannot be expelled, even if they are known.

Satan also tried to sow his tare in the heart of Peter. He tried to do so after God gave the revelation of who Jesus is to him. Jesus had asked the disciples what men say that He, the Son of Man, is. They had answered that some say that He is John the Baptist: some, Elijah; and others, Jeremiah, or one of the prophets. He then asked them who they say that He is. It was Simon Peter who answered the important question. He said, "You are the Christ, the Son of the Living God" (Matthew 16:16).

Jesus answered and said unto him, "Blessed are you, Simon Bar-Jonah, for flesh and blood has not revealed *this* to you, but My Father who is in heaven. And I also say to you that you are Peter, and on this rock I will build My church, and the gates of Hades shall not prevail against it" (Matthew 16:17–18). What is the importance of this revelation by the Father and of the declaration by the Lord Jesus Christ? I presume that God the Father virtually appointed Peter there and then as a future leader of the disciples. This is because the Scripture says, "A man can receive nothing unless it has been given to him from heaven" (John 3:27).

We can now see the Father giving a staff of authority and leadership to Peter among them. Jesus then affirmed this action of the Father by saying, "And I will give you the keys of the kingdom of heaven, and whatever you bind on earth will be bound in heaven, and whatever you loose on earth will be loosed in heaven" (Matthew 16:19).

This public proclamation and promotion of Peter among the disciples certainly drew the attention of Satan to him. After all, it is said in Zechariah 13:7, "Strike the Shepherd, and the sheep shall be scattered?" If he could get at Peter, he could then succeed to a large extent to destroy the work of the Kingdom of God that Jesus would hand over to the disciples.

I hope that the reader would remember that after the crucifixion of Jesus, Peter only needed to announce that he was going to fish and six other disciples readily followed him! They almost abandoned the work of the Kingdom of God. Jesus had to pay them one more visit at the place where they had gone to fish. He particularly focused on converting Peter at this event (John 21:15–17). He succeeded.

It was Peter who later rose up to fill the leadership vacuum which the exit of Jesus created following His ascension. The Scripture describes his assumption of leadership thus, "And in those days Peter stood up in the midst of the disciples, and said… men *and* brethren, this Scripture had to be fulfilled, which the Holy Spirit spoke before by the mouth of David concerning Judas, who became a guide to those who arrested Jesus" (Acts 1:15–16).

Satan Failed to Sow Peter as Tare

It was immediately after promoting Peter that Jesus began to show His disciples why He must go unto Jerusalem. There in Jerusalem He shall suffer many things of the elders and chief priests and scribes. He will eventually be killed. But on the third day He shall be raised again. It was Peter that began to rebuke Him for His utterance. He said in particular, "Far be it from You, Lord; this shall not happen to You!" This was how Satan, the Devil, tried to sow his tare in the heart of Peter.

The Master who knew where the rebuke by Peter was coming from addressed the source squarely. He charged at him who had taken temporary residence in Peter and was using his mouth to make ungodly suggestion: "Get behind Me, Satan! You are an offence to Me, for you are not mindful of the things of God, but the things of men." Satan successfully sowed his tare in Judas Iscariot. He also "sowed" him in the midst of the disciples. He, however, failed to sow his tare in Peter.

Satan, however, did not give up the desire to get at Peter. This was despite being rebuked by Jesus during his temporary occupation of him. He later desired to have Peter and sift him as wheat. What gave Satan the audacity to desire to do so?

Peter's thoughts and words were later responsible for Satan's desire. Peter had thought that the battle before Jesus could be won by physical might and power. He was, therefore, relying on the might and power of flesh to help Jesus. He even said that he was ready to go with Jesus into prison and also lay down his life for His sake.

He thought that he could do these by his might and power. That thought indicates pride. The Scripture, however, says, "Pride goes before destruction, and a haughty spirit before a fall" (Proverbs 16:18). Peter did not know that the battle before Jesus could only be fought and won by the Spirit of the LORD of hosts (Zechariah 4:6).

Violation of those divine laws by Peter was what gave Satan the audacity to desire from God to sift him as wheat. Because Jesus knows all that take place in the spiritual realm, He saw the clandestine moves of Satan. Jesus thus exposed the plot of Satan in these words, "...Simon, Simon! Indeed, Satan has asked for you, that he may sift you as wheat: but I have prayed for you, that your faith should not fail; and when you have returned to *Me*, strengthen your brethren" (Luke 22:31–32). That last part of the text in King James' Version says, when you have been converted, strengthen your brethren.

Jesus then told Peter that he would deny Him three times before the cock crowed. This was when Peter spoke out what Satan already knew about him and for which he had desired to sift him. He disputed the prediction of the Master. He was still relying on his might and power. He later shamefully denied his Master three times. He learnt a bitter lesson: the unreliability of the flesh. He wept, but it was the prior prayer of Jesus that saved him.

Declaration of a Spiritual Battle

The parable of the wheat and tare served as a declaration of war. Jesus declared by the parable in the public arena a spiritual war. The spiritual war is between the Kingdom of Light and the kingdom of darkness. While the Unseen Father put Jesus forward as His representative in the ensuing battles, the unseen Satan put Judas Iscariot forward as his. The Father and Satan were inside of Jesus Christ and Judas Iscariot respectively.

Discerning readers of the Bible would note that after the series of parables according to the record of Matthew, Jesus went to His home town, Nazareth. He taught in their synagogue. They were astonished at His doctrine. They wondered where He got the wisdom from. They were also astonished at the miracles He wrought. What should be expected of those folks in view of their correct observations? I suppose that it should be to believe in Him so as to be saved. But what followed?

Number One: they derided Him by describing Him as the carpenter's (Joseph's) son and not as the Son of God. Number Two: they derided Him by describing Him more as Mary's son, and less as the Son of God. Number Three: they derided Him by listing the names of His brothers and sisters. This way, they regarded Him just as an ordinary fellow, the guy of the next block that came to the world by no special means. This was how they rejected His supernatural conception and personality. Finally, Number Four: they were offended in Him. All these boil down to rejection of Him as their Savior from sins and eternal death.

From the analyses thus far, dear reader, you would clearly see that Satan started in earnest to try to discredit Him. But Jesus simply replied thus: "A prophet is not without honor, except in his own country and in his own house" (Matthew 13:57). The sad result of their attitude was that "…He did not do many mighty works there because of their unbelief."

It was not that He could not do mighty works. Instead, it was that He didn't do many mighty works there. Such works as raising the dead could be done through His compassion or through the belief of the person or people involved. Both were exemplified by raising the dead son of the widow of Nain and the daughter of Jairus, a ruler of a synagogue. But He only laid hand on a few sick folks to heal them (Mark 6:5). It was a great loss that they suffered because of their unbelief!

Judas Iscariot Was Uprooted by Death

The identification of Judas Iscariot as the seed of Satan takes us far back into the Old Testament. The serpent had successfully deceived Eve to eat the forbidden fruit of the tree of the knowledge of good and evil. Adam

So the main issue is not when one eventually believes but that the person ultimately believes before he physically dies, which is the first death.

had joined his wife in the act by eating the fruit which she presented to him. All the characters involved had to be judged. The judgment is described in Genesis 3:15 (KJV). The LORD God said, "And I will put enmity between you and the woman, and between your seed and her Seed; it shall bruise your head, and you shall bruise His heel." Judas Iscariot was that seed of the serpent. He thus came to perform his role in an eternal program, just as Jesus, the Seed of the woman, also came to perform His.[6]

Jesus did not uproot the tare, Judas Iscariot, from among the disciples; even though He knew that he was a planting of His enemy, the Devil. He allowed him to remain with the others until the end of his life which happened by suicide. If He had uprooted him midway, the fault might have been placed at His door step. For example, Satan might have accused Him of refusing to save him by excommunicating him. He could have charged Him with negligence. After all, he could have said, "He claimed that He came to seek and to save that which was lost. Why did He excommunicate him instead of saving him?" But the principle of God is, "Let both grow together until the harvest…" (Matthew 13:30).

By allowing him to continue with the others unto the end, Satan could not blame Jesus for his fate. Judas Iscariot had nobody to blame but himself. He said, "I have sinned in that I have betrayed the innocent blood." The Jewish leaders answered, "What *is that* to us? See you to that." He cast down the pieces of silver in the temple, departed and hanged himself (Matthew 27:1–5). "He went from frying pan into fire," so to say. This shows that Jesus would tolerate every evil plot until such a plotter dies. No wonder, "…It is appointed for men to die once, but after this the judgment" (Hebrews 9:27). In the same way, Jesus allows the witches and wizards to congregate together in His Church <u>until the harvest</u>.

[6] Adeoye, Adedeji David: *Jesus and the Trinity: What Many Believers Don't Know,* [Page Turner Press and Media LLC, 601 E., Palomar St., Suite c-478, Chula Vista, CA 91911, USA, 2018.]

The final word of Judas Iscariot was confession of evil done and condemnation of self. This further confirms that Jesus did not come to condemn anybody, but to save mankind. For example, He said to the woman that was caught in adultery, in the very act, "Neither do I condemn you; go and sin no more" (John 8:11).

The story of Judas Iscariot ended the way it did to show that Satan cannot be saved. And like Judas Iscariot regretted at the end of his ungodly acts, so will Satan. And the lesson to learn by every Tom, Dick and Harry is that whoever sides with Satan should be ready to suffer the same fate as Judas Iscariot suffered. Such people will not hear the voice of the Son of God. They would, therefore, be separated from God. This is what it means to fail to live after the first and second death (John 5:25, 29). They would be damned.

Another lesson to learn derives from Matthew 15:13. It says, "But He answered and said, 'Every plant which My heavenly Father has not planted, will be uprooted.'" Judas Iscariot was not the planting of God the Father but of Satan, the Devil. He was thus uprooted. It is who is being planted by the Father that can cause the sort of statement that is credited to Apostle John in 1 John 3:9. It says, "Whoever has been born of God does not sin, for His seed remains in him; and he cannot sin, because he has been born of God."

Judas Iscariot eventually became the only disciple that was unfruitful. He ended his life in perdition, that the Scripture might be fulfilled (John 17:12). It is note-worthy that both the Parable of the Sower and that of the Wheat and Tare are interpreted by Jesus. This is to enable us to clearly understand their importance and thereby learn from them.

Jesus, certainly, knew how long it would take to get Thomas Didymus to believe in Him and at what time. His belief in Jesus eventually happened after His resurrection, following another visit to the disciples. So the main issue is not when one eventually believes but that the person ultimately believes before he physically dies, which is the first death. This first death amounts to separation from Jesus, while the second death amounts to separation from God the Father.

Despite this general knowledge, Jesus made a special call. He says, "Come to Me, all *you* who labor and are heavy laden, and I will give you rest. Take My yoke upon you, and learn from Me, for I am gentle and lowly in heart, and you will find rest for your souls. For My yoke *is* easy and My burden is light" (Matthew 11:28–30). Those who desire rest for their souls must believe also in Him. His capacity to know all things recommends Him as an additional Person to believe in also. The benefit is eternal life with Him, the Father, the holy angels, and saints of God in heaven.

CHAPTER 6

Establishment of Judaism

A Common Background

Jesus acknowledged that the disciples believed in God. It was their belief in God that motivated them to come to Him, following the testimonies they heard about Him. These disciples were, therefore, coming from a common background. And that background, by the way, was not limited to them. It was also common to the Israelites that came out of the background of the fatherhood of Abraham, God's friend forever (2 Chronicles 20:7; Isaiah 41:8; James 2:23).

The Jews readily acknowledged Abraham as their father. Some of them of the days of Jesus, during a controversy with Him, said, "... Abraham is our father.... We are not born of fornication; we have one Father, even God" (John 8:39, 41). How do we describe this background from which the Jews were coming other than being "religious?" They recognized God as the object of their creation, confession, and worship.

It was religion, therefore, that was at the background of their belief in God. It was that background that gave the disciples the initial push to believe the testimonies about Jesus the Messiah, Christ, the Son of the living God.

The giving of the Ten Commandments, on which God's covenant with Israel is based, was carried out in a very special atmosphere. There were thunderings, lightnings, noises of trumpets, and the smokes of the mountain. It was such that when the people saw them, they were afraid. They then said unto Moses, "You speak with us, and we will hear; but let not God speak with us, lest we die" [Exodus 20:19]. The religion which originated from these violent atmospheric eruptions became known as Judaism. Because of the people's fear of dying from these occurrences, that religion can be assumed to possess the potential to kill.

After the violent atmospheric eruptions, which were accompanied with the noise of trumpets subsided, God invited the elders to the top of the mount. There is a lot to learn about how to approach God from what followed this invitation.

God demanded worship from them before they could come up to Him on the Mount. Therefore, they built an altar and twelve pillars according to the twelve tribes of Israel under the hill. They worshipped God with burnt and peace offerings. Moses sprinkled half of the blood collected from the offerings on the altar. He then read the terms of the Covenant to the people. They pledged to obey the terms of the covenant. Moses then sprinkled the remaining half of the blood on the people.

God accepted their worship which consisted of the protocols that they meticulously carried out. He then welcomed them to His presence on the Mount. The fellowship was celebrated with eating and drinking. He also confirmed His acceptance of their worship by not laying hand on them. This means that He did not kill them. The big lesson to learn from these protocols shall be addressed at the end of this chapter.

After the fellowship, God invited Moses back to the top of the Mount. He left the elders at the foot of the hill. Joshua, however, escorted him part of the way to God. Moses was with God on Mount Sinai for forty days. At the end of the lengthy period, two stone tables on which the Ten Commandments were inscribed by God were ready. The first of the Ten Commandments was that the people were not to have any other gods before Him. They were not to make unto themselves any graven image, or any likeness of anything that is in heaven above, or that is in the earth beneath, or that is in the water under the earth. They were not to bow down themselves to them, or serve them (Exodus 20:3–5). The LORD God was to be their only object of belief, confession, and worship. And they were to constantly recognize Him as the LORD God that brought them out of the Egyptian bondage.

But just before Moses was to descend from the mount, Aaron and the other leaders had given up on Moses returning. They, therefore, fashioned a god of a calf as a replacement for the living God. Aaron presented the molten calf to the people as the god that brought them out of Egypt. He also built an altar before it. He then proclaimed the following day to be a feast to the LORD (Exodus 32:5).

God told Moses five things that Aaron and the other leaders had done. First, they had turned aside quickly out of the way which God commanded them. Second, they had made for themselves a molten calf. Third, they had worshipped the molten calf. Fourth, they had sacrificed unto it; and fifth, they had confessed that it was the calf that brought them out of Egypt (Exodus 32:8). God was displeased with the actions of Aaron and the people and was ready to replace them with a new set of people through Moses.

God later regarded Moses as the very meek (humble) above all the men which were upon the face of the earth (Numbers 12:3). I think that it was because Moses did not grab the offer of God to replace the Israelites with new seed from him that made God to so regard him. Instead, he interceded for them and God accepted his intercession and continued to tolerate them.

Moses and Joshua came down from the mountain on the same day that they chose to celebrate their new god with feasting and dancing. When Moses saw what they had invented, he felt more disappointed than God. Two things were simultaneously broken that day. First, the people broke the first law in the list of the Ten Commandments under the leadership of Aaron. Second, Moses broke the two tables of the Law into pieces. Literally, the "establishment" of the worship of the golden calf and the Living God took place simultaneously.

As mentioned in Chapter 2, Moses asked those that were still on the side of the LORD God to come over to him. Only the tribe of Levi from the third son of Jacob did. He then ordered them to draw their swords and execute the judgment of God by killing every man his brother, companion, and neighbor. At the end of carrying out the judgment, 3,000 people had been slain.

The worship of the Living God was inaugurated by the Almighty God through Moses. It was on the same day that the worship of idols was inaugurated by the elders through Aaron. It was done with feasting and dancing. That Aaron committed a serious sin was not in doubt. It was, however, the same man that God later ordained to be the high priest to minister in God's tabernacle. This was an indication of God's readiness to forgive man his sins if he has someone to intercede for him as Moses did for Aaron and the people (Exodus 32:12; Deuteronomy 9:20).

Moses went up with two new tables of stone which he hewed at God's instruction. They were like fake ones when compared with those which God hewed and wrote upon by Himself but which Moses broke. God again wrote on them the Ten Commandments. Moses was on Mount Sinai with God for another period of forty days. By the time he was descending from the presence of the LORD God with the two new stone tables of the Ten Commandments, his face shone. He had had a transfer of God's glory unto his face.

Consequently, it became dangerous for the people to look at his face when holding a meeting with him. In order to avoid destroying the eyes of the people, Moses had to start wearing a veil to cover his face. With time, however, the shining effect of the glory of God on his face faded. But it was like he had so overly enjoyed the excitement of being seen as special by being the only man that was wearing a veil. Therefore, though the shining glory wore off over time, Moses did not remove the veil whenever he met with the congregation of the LORD.

His continual action of wearing a veil was thus rather dishonest. Dishonesty is a sin.

Apostle Paul, commented on the veil of Moses which he only put off whenever he went up to appear before the LORD on the mountain (Exodus 34:34). He says, "Unlike Moses, *who* put a veil over his face so that the children of Israel could not look steadily at the end of what was passing away. But their minds were blinded. For until this day the same veil remains unlifted in the reading of the Old Testament, because the *veil* is taken away in Christ" (2 Corinthians 3:13–14). Through this practice, Moses "blinded" the minds of readers of the Old Testament Scripture. It became a defect in Judaism which persisted even until today.

We have seen that it was God that gave the Jews the Law through Moses. He also gave several prophecies through several prophets. The prophets are described as either major or minor. Those with long writings are described as major while those with short are described as minor. It was also by God's directive that the priesthood was established.

God was also the One that gave the specifications of the dresses of the priests. He also gave the detailed specifications of the tabernacle/sanctuary, the place of sacrifice. It was a pattern of the true tabernacle in heaven. Inside them, the priests ministered. The tabernacle consisted of the outer court which contained the brazen altar for burnt offering. The brazen altar was located at the entrance point in the outer court. The outer court also had the laver which contained water. With the water in the laver, the priest purified himself before going further into the holy place which is the middle court.

The holy place is separated with a curtain from the outer court. The holy place contained a table of showbread and a candlestick. It was also separated from the third compartment, the holiest of all, with a curtain. The Ark of Covenant was in this third compartment. In the Ark of Covenant was a specimen of the manna, a sample of the food of angels, with which God fed the people in the wilderness. Inside the Ark of Covenant there were also the two tables of stone of the Ten Commandments. The last item was the dry rod of Aaron which budded. The budding of the rod was a proof that he was the one whom God chose as the high priest among the other children of Levi who later contested the office with him.

The Ark of Covenant was overlaid with gold. On top of it was the mercy seat. It was flanked with two cherubims with wings stretched towards each other to cover the seat. In a nutshell, everything was built as per the pattern that God showed to Moses on Mount Sinai.

It was by all these – the Ten Commandments, tabernacle and sanctuary, utensils, and dresses for the priests – that the religion of the Jews, Judaism, and its attendant practices were established. Judaism, the religion of the Jews, thus enjoyed divine origin in the Old Testament period. But, the law is weak through the flesh (Romans 8:3) hence the people could not obey them. Therefore, the law could not save. Its ability to save is further hampered by the pretense which Moses introduced into it. This resulted from his continual practice of wearing the veil which had lost its value.

The Veil Was Done Away with In Christ

The veil that Moses occasionally wore should have been done away with when the glory that shone on his face had faded. The faded glory could have helped the people to realize that Judaism could not save. But, no, he continued to wear it on his face. The veil eventually transmuted into a covering over the face of the children of Israel when they read the Old Testament.

The Scripture says, "By the mouth of two or three witnesses every word may be established" (Matthew 18:16; John 8:17; 2 Corinthians 13:1). Jesus and Paul established the truth of the veil not being taken away in the reading of the Old Testament.

It was by the encounter of Moses with God on Mount Sinai that he started wearing a veil. Paul bore witness to this veil by the Spirit of the Lord as noted above. It was also by the specification of God that a veil or curtain was placed between the holy place and the holy of holies. A replica of the veil was in the temple that King Solomon constructed. It was also installed in the temple that King Herod constructed. Jesus taught the people a number of times in the temple of Herod. It was from it that He drove away, with whip, sellers and buyers of wares. They had effectively converted the place meant for prayer and worship to a market and a den of thieves.

Prophet Isaiah says about it, "Even them I will bring to My holy mountain, and make them joyful in My house of prayer. Their burnt offerings and their sacrifices *will be* accepted on My altar; for My house shall be called a house of prayer for all nations" (Isaiah 56:7).

Only the high priest had access into the holiest of all once in a year to make atonement. The priest will first make atonement for himself; he will then make atonement for the people. It was out of bounds to anybody apart from the high priest. Whenever it was time for the priest to go into the holiest compartment for the annual ministration, a chain was normally tied to his ankle. Small bells were also tied to the hem of his dress. The bells would jingle as he moved from place to place while performing religious rites (Luke 1:8–10). It showed that he was still alive. If the bells stopped jingling, which might indicate that he had died, having been slain for possibly violating a command of God, the chain would be used to drag him out. Therefore, there was the fear in every minister that he might not come out alive from the sanctuary.

The veil that Moses occasionally wore should have been done away with when the glory that shone on his face had faded. The faded glory could have helped the people to realize that Judaism could not save.

Nadab and Abihu were the first two of the four sons of Aaron, the high priest. They were also priests in their own right. They were privileged to be among those that went up the mount to meet with God. They suffered such a sudden death. This happened when they took their censers and offered strange fire in the holiest tabernacle. Fire came down from God and consumed them. Aaron lost two sons in one day.

A different example was the case of King Uzziah who, out of pride, tried to burn incense in the temple. This was an assignment which he was not qualified for. God reserved the assignment for the Levites. By trespassing, God struck him with leprosy on his forehead (2 Chronicles 26:19–21). He died a leper like Gehazi, the servant of Prophet Elisha.

It was inside this compartment that angel Gabriel appeared to Zechariah, the husband of Elizabeth. He gave him the good news of the promise of a son to be born in their old age. He was to be called John. Even though he did not believe the good news because of his old age, it came to pass. For daring to ask, "How shall I know this?" he was given the sign of dumbness. He thus remained dumb until the child was born and was to be circumcised on the eighth day.

The elders called him Zechariah, but the mother, Elizabeth, objected. She insisted on calling him John. They said that there was nobody ever called by that name in the lineage. They, however, did well to make a sign to Zechariah over how he would have him called. He requested for a writing table. They gave him. As he wrote "John", his mouth was opened immediately, and his tongue loosed, and he spoke, and praised God.

The second witness was Jesus. Through Him, the veil was miraculously removed. This happened when He uttered His last statement on the cross before He gave up the ghost. The scripture says, "And Jesus cried out again with a loud voice, and yielded up His spirit (ghost)" (Matthew 27:50). The last words He uttered which is recorded in John 19:30 are, "It is finished!" At that very instant, according to Matthew 27:51–52; Mark 15:38; and Luke 23:45, the record says, "… Behold, the veil of the temple was torn in two from top to the bottom; and the earth quaked…." This was how the veil was done away with in Christ.

Moses practically and unintentionally perfected the veil of religion which prevents the adherents of Judaism from understanding the Scripture. This is because it is through the words of Jesus that we can understand the Old Testament Scripture. Hence, He said, loud and clear, that He did not come to destroy the law, or the prophets: but to fulfill (Matthew 5:17). The leadership rejected Jesus. They also, virtually, rejected all that had to do with Him. They are, therefore, still expecting their Messiah to come despite His resurrection and ascension to heaven.

Promise of a Prophet

Another significant thing followed the desire of the people to have Moses speak with them, instead of God, lest they die. The significant thing was that God unfolded His plan to send them a prophet like Moses. Moses states the plan thus: "The LORD your God will raise up for you a Prophet like me from your midst, from your brethren. Him you shall hear, according to all that you desired of the LORD your God in Horeb in the day of the assembly, saying, 'Let me not hear again the voice of the LORD my God, nor let me see this great fire anymore, lest I die" (Deuteronomy 18:15–16).

From this Scripture, it is evident that the segment that says, "…a Prophet from your midst, from your brethren…" refers to the entire nation of Israel. The noun, "brethren," means "brothers." In this context, it refers to the twelve sons of Jacob who became the twelve tribes of Israel. Of these tribes, it was the tribe of Judah that Jacob, the third patriarch from Abraham, had prophetically allotted the kingship. He declared it thus: "Judah, you *are he* whom your brothers shall praise…."

Therefore, the next segment that says, "...of your brothers ..." refers to the tribe of Judah out of the twelve brothers that comprised the twelve tribes (Genesis 49:8–12).

The explanation that the noun "brothers" refers to "tribes" is confirmed in Deuteronomy 18:1–2. The text says, "The priests, the Levites–and all the tribe of Levi–shall have no part or inheritance with Israel.... Therefore they shall have no inheritance among their brethren; the LORD *is* their inheritance, as He said to them." The noun, "brethren," thus refers to "tribes." And it was from the tribe of Judah that Jesus eventually emerged as has been pointed out earlier.

Two comments shall be made on the subsequent response of God to the request of the Israelites in the wilderness. The first comment is that the content of Deuteronomy 18:15–16 is a reported or indirect speech. Moses reported the plan that the LORD God had in His mind for the young nation of Israel and, by extension, for all the other nations of the world. The LORD God whose plan Moses reported is God the Father. He is the God whose voice no one in the Old Testament, including Adam, Noah, Abraham, and Moses ever heard. Apostle John says, "No one has seen God at any time. The only begotten Son, who is in the bosom of the Father, He has declared Him" (John 1:18). This truth is also corroborated by Jesus. He said, "...You have neither heard His voice at any time, nor seen His form" (John 5:37).

> Judaism, the religion of the Old Testament era, was established in a very special atmosphere. It was named after Judah, whose name means "praise."

The second comment is that it is not that God the Father cannot speak. He is not like the gods fashioned out of gold, wood, stone, and iron that cannot speak. It is just that He hardly speaks. This is because

He had given His word a voice. This truth is confirmed in Psalm 103:20. It says, "Bless the Lord, you His angels, who excel in strength, who do His word, heeding the voice of His word." Jesus, the Godhead bodily (Colossians 2:8–9), is the voice of the Word of God the Father.

John 3:34 says, "For He whom God has sent speaks the words of God, for God does not give the Spirit by measure *unto Him."* Jesus is the one being referred to in that Scripture. It was when He was being baptized in River Jordan by John the Baptist that God gave Him His Spirit without measure. The Spirit descended visibly like a dove, and perched upon Him. Jesus, the voice of the Word of the Father, was the one to be introduced on three different occasions in the New Testament. The introduction was to make Him known as the Promised Prophet. The Father had to speak out directly, for no one of lesser status, on this notable occasion, could introduce Him.

The first time He spoke out directly in the Gospels was when John baptized Him. The Father spoke out of the open heaven to introduce Him when He went up straightway out of the water. The Father said, "This is My beloved Son, in whom I am well pleased" (Matthew 3:17).

The second time the Father spoke was on the Mount of Transfiguration. He introduced Jesus again, saying, "This is My beloved Son, in whom I am well pleased. Hear Him" (Matthew 17:5). This introduction served to enable the three disciples, Peter, James, and John to know that Jesus is far above Moses and Elijah in rank. It was at this event that the Father also introduced Jesus as His Word which had taken on the shape of a Person. This He did by directing the disciples to "hear Him".

The third time that the Father spoke out directly and was heard, the crucifixion of Jesus was imminent. Jesus declared publicly as recorded in John 12:27, "Now My soul is troubled, and what shall I say? 'Father, save Me from this hour? But for this purpose I came to this hour.'" He then prayed a very short prayer: "Father, glorify Your name." At this juncture, a voice from heaven was heard saying, "I have both glorified *it,* and will glorify it again" (John 12:28). So, the voice that was heard was that of the Father to whom Jesus had prayed.

Some people, who were around Jesus at the time, heard the voice. Those who heard it said that it thundered. Others said that an angel spoke to Him. But Jesus declared, "This voice did not come because of Me, but for your sake" (John 12:30). The voice that came was that of the Father whose name Jesus had requested Him to glorify. Therefore, in the New Testament, the voice of the Father had been heard three times. But this was because there was no one of higher ranking in heaven qualified to introduce the Son to mankind on these three occasions other than the Father.

There is no shape to see other than the physical appearance of Jesus. Whoever has seen Jesus has seen the Father. This is because the Father is in the Son (John 14:9–11). This is also because the Father is "the Soul of God," and Jesus is "the Body of God."

The above scenarios were enacted so as to convince the public that Jesus is that Promised Prophet. They should then be ready to hearken unto God's words which He (Jesus) had all along been voicing, otherwise, the Father would require it of them (Deuteronomy 18:19; John 12:30). If the Father would require it of that generation, He will not do less with ours.

The Big Lesson to Learn

We have learnt from the episode at the foot of Mount Sinai that worship through sacrifice is necessary before one can approach God. Had they not offered the due sacrifices, with the attendant sprinkling of blood, they would not have had access to God on the Mount. The big lesson to learn is that it is by the precious blood of His only begotten Son that we can come into His presence. It is while we are still alive on earth that we can make the necessary decision to believe in Him and be saved. And if Judaism with its supernatural origin could not save from sin, such that Jesus had to be given, it follows that any other religion cannot.

PART IV

The Third Segment of John 14:1: ...Believe also in Me."

This part consists of six chapters. They show how Jesus qualified to be the Savior and to being expected to come the second time.

Commandment is in the form of dos and don'ts. It gives birth to religion such as Judaism with accompanying rituals. Commandment, however, could not save man from the sin which makes every person to be short of the glory of God (Romans 3:23). Therefore, every person that dies in sin cannot enter into the kingdom of God.

It is when a person dies in a pool of water that he can be said to have drowned. Similarly, it is when a man dies without having been saved that he can be said to have died in sin. And, just like it is a good swimmer that can rescue a man that is drowning, so also is it a sinless person that can rescue a man that is drowning in sin.

Every person is drowning in sin. Therefore, each person should not continue to hope that his or her religion will take him or her to God, only to be disappointed at the end. Hence, the compelling need to "believe also in Jesus," who is the Savior which God gave to the world (John 3:16).

CHAPTER 7

God and Jesus

Foundation or Substructure and Superstructure

John 14:1 says, "Let not your heart be troubled; you believe in God, believe also in Me." The first three-letter word, "Let", shows that the disciples whom Jesus was addressing were to choose to prevent their heart from being troubled. What you choose, if you are given, and you receive it, is what you have. So, by the choice of the disciples, the Spirit of the LORD of hosts will enable them to believe also in Jesus.

The emphasis or weight of their belief, by which their heart would be prevented from being troubled, is thus on Jesus, and not God, per se. This is because they already believed in God, yet Jesus still commanded them not to let their hearts be troubled. It is their belief in God that provides the solid foundation or substructure, upon which their belief in Jesus can rest.

The foundation of a building is not a comfortable place to reside on. It is open to inclement weather. Belief in Jesus is like the superstructure which is finely completed for lodging. It is no wonder that Jesus promised to go and prepare a place for the disciples in the Father's kingdom. After preparing a place for them, He would then come back to receive each disciple unto Himself in his comfortable mansion (John 14:2–3). The two of them, God and Jesus, therefore, work together as the foundation and the superstructure of a building do. The foundation and the superstructure are very necessary for a comfortable abode. And, as the foundation is under the ground level and is thus invisible, so is God. The superstructure, on the other hand, is above the ground level and visible. So is Jesus.

Three basic conclusions are derivable from this analogy. The first is that when the saints get to heaven, they may not see God. This is because He will be acting as the hidden foundation of His house. He, however, will be the One carrying the mansions which the saints shall be dwelling in. The second is that the saints will see Jesus. This is because He will be acting as the superstructure, which is not hidden. He will be providing the various rooms in the mansions. The third is that all the saints will then be dwelling in both God and Jesus. What a secure place to be after all the toils and troubles on earth!

Before dwelling in those mansions in heaven, however, the saints can have a taste of them on earth. This is what Jesus alluded to when He said, "If anyone loves Me, he will keep My words; and My Father will love him, and We will come to him and make Our home with him" (John 14:23). The home of God and Jesus on earth consists of God as its foundation, and Jesus as its superstructure. The saints can thus dwell securely in them on earth before relocating to heaven far away from the presence of sin.

The righteousness that a man displays at the level of belief in God, or Judaism, or any religion for that matter, is, at best, like filthy rags. Prophet Isaiah says, "But we are all like an unclean *thing,* and all our righteousnesses *are* like filthy rags, we all fade as a leaf, and our iniquities, like the wind, have taken us away" (Isaiah 64:6). We, therefore, need the righteousness of Jesus to dwell in that beautiful city with its street of pure gold (Revelation 21:21).

Four Preliminary Periods of Man

In Romans 7:9, Apostle Paul says, "I was alive once without the law, but when the commandment came, sin revived and I died." This Scripture can be divided into four preliminary periods of man. The first period says, "I was alive once without the law...." This first period is as a child who could, without shame, go out unclothed. In this period, he does not harbor any ill feelings against any one. He is absolutely innocent. He has no room for malice in his heart against anyone (1 Corinthians 14:20).

The second period says, "…But when the commandment came…." This is when the child reaches the age of accountability. He now knows what constitute "Dos" and "Don'ts." "Dos" and "Don'ts" make up the commandments. This is followed with the third period which says, "… sin revived…."

This very short statement shows that sin which had been dormant in the flesh comes fully alive and starts to hold sway. The characteristic of this period is the struggle to obey the commandments. Unfortunately, the power to obey them is absent. This is because the commandment or law has been weakened through the flesh (Romans 8:3). Hence, the child that had become an adult could not obey it. This is what results in the fourth period which says, "…and I died." The man that was born into belief in God, which includes the religion of his parents, such as Judaism, becomes spiritually dead.

It will be remembered that the shining effect of the glory of God on the face of Moses faded over time. It did not go "from glory to glory." Rather it went "from glory to pretense." This is what happens when one had been in the position of "you believe in God" by birth. Rather than continue in pretense, it is a righteous act at such a time, to ask for help. And the help is readily available at the level of "Believe also in Jesus."

This is how God shows His divine love, grace, and mercy. He does by providing the means whereby the adherent of the religion into which he was born, but in which he becomes dead, could be helped. The man can then accomplish his destiny, which I describe as being able to return to the Father at the end like Jesus did. I wonder why someone would neglect such a precious lifeline that God has graciously thrown to him! This could only be through lack of belief or faith in

Jesus. Neglecting this lone lifeline is a decision or choice to perish. This is what it amounts to for any man that refuses to submit to spiritual conversion. It is an act of wisdom to hold unto the only lifeline, the Son of God, whom God has given to the world. It is by Him alone that anyone can enter into God's Kingdom and not by religion.

Jesus made this truth manifest when He told Nicodemus, "For God so loved the world, that He gave His only begotten Son, that whoever believes in Him should not perish, but have everlasting life. For God did not send His Son into the world to condemn the world, but *(is)* that the world through Him might be saved. He who believes in Him is not condemned; but he who does not believe is condemned already, because he has not believed in the name of the only begotten Son of God. And this is the condemnation, that the light has come into the world, and men loved darkness rather than light, because their deeds were evil. For every one practising evil hates the light and does not come to the light, lest his deeds should be exposed. But he who does the truth comes to the light, that his deeds may be clearly seen, that they have been done in God" (John 3:16–21).

Acceptance of Jesus should be the glorious concluding prime decision of every person that comes to the world.

Apostle Paul confirms this position in Romans 7:10–17. He says, "And the commandment, which *was* to *bring* life, I found *to bring* death. For sin, taking occasion by the commandment, deceived me, and by it killed *me.* Therefore the law is holy, and the commandment holy and just, and good. Has then what is good become death to me? Certainly not! But sin, that it might appear sin, was producing death in me through what is good, so that sin through the commandment might become exceedingly sinful. For we know that the law is spiritual, but I am carnal, sold under sin. For what I am doing, I do not understand. For what I will to do, that I do not practise; but what I hate, that I do. If then I do that which I would not, I agree with the law that *it is* good. But now, *it is* no longer I who do it, but sin that dwells in me."

The summary of that Scripture is that the commandment by which religion came was supposed to bring life to mankind; instead it brought death. And this is because, fundamentally, Jesus is the Savior and not religion. Religion cannot save. Only Jesus who is the Way to the Father is the One that can save and does save.

My concluding comment on this scriptural submission is simple. It is only the blood of Jesus that is empowered to cleanse the sin in everybody who finds himself or herself by birth on earth and in religion. Acceptance of Jesus should be the glorious concluding prime decision of every person that comes to the world.

Jesus Spoke from the Premise of Knowledge

Jesus continued His final words thus, "In My Father's house are many mansions: if *it* were not *so*, I would have told you" (John 14:2). Jesus did not speak from the premise of faith in that verse, but of knowledge. We should remember that He told Nicodemus the night he visited Him, "Are you the teacher of Israel, and do not *know* (italics for emphasis) these things? Most assuredly, I say unto you, 'We speak what We *know* (italics for emphasis), and testify what we have seen, and you do not receive Our witness. If I have told you earthly things, and you do not believe, how will you believe, if I tell you heavenly things?" (John 3:10–12). It is the role of the disciples to believe what He tells them; just like He required Nicodemus to do.

The Father's House

The Father's house can be defined as the kingdom of God. This definition can be confirmed by comparing Scripture with Scripture. Hophni and Phinehas were committing sin in the sanctuary in Shiloh. God then sent a man to announce to Eli, their father, his punishment for failing to reprimand them. In 1 Samuel 2:27, God asked Eli, "…

Did I not clearly reveal Myself to the house of your father, when they were in Egypt in Pharaoh's house?"

The statement "when they were in Egypt in Pharaoh's house" does not mean that the Israelites dwelt in the house of Pharaoh when they were in Egypt. Instead, they dwelt in his kingdom or domain, a part of it that was called Goshen. The phrase "the house of Pharaoh" would then mean "the kingdom of Pharaoh." The Father's house, therefore, means the Kingdom of God. Jesus then announced His next assignment to the disciples. It is to go and prepare a place for them in the Kingdom of God. He then followed it up with a number of promises.

The first promise is to come again. This promise was confirmed by two men who wore white apparel and stood by the disciples when He ascended back into heaven. They said, "This same Jesus, who was taken up from you into heaven, will so come in like manner as you saw Him go into heaven" (Acts 1:11). The second promise is to receive them unto Himself. This is as a bridegroom receives the bride to himself during a wedding ceremony. The third promise is to have them be with Him.

The "Where" and the "Way" Are Known

Jesus continued and said, "And where I go you know, and the way, you know" (John 14:4). But Thomas, one of His disciples, countered, saying, "Lord, we do not know where You are going, and how can we know the way?"

The "where" that He was going to was known by all the disciples. This was because it was on the basis of their belief in God that they had come to Him in the first place. The only constraint that they had at that time, however, was that they had not yet believed that it was God the Father that sent Him.

Jesus said, "And where I go you know…." Jesus was going back to the Father. This was because it was the Father that sent Him to the world. They did so by believing the record of Moses and the prophets about

Him. Jesus had also acknowledged that the disciples believe in God. He, therefore, came forth from the Father, and He would also return to Him. This is because it is the person that sends someone on an errand that one returns to, at the end of one's mission, to give account.

Whoever goes to hell after death does so from the platform of belief in God without also believing in Jesus, for He is the only way to God. It will be the outcome of tragic carelessness

Jesus also said, "And the way you know." The disciples knew the way to the Father because they knew Jesus who is the way to the Father. Jesus also knew that they knew Him, at least physically. The only constraint that they had was that they had not believed in Him. Hence, He asked them to believe also in Him. He, then, unequivocally, introduced Himself as the Way, the Truth, and the Life. No one can come to the Father except through Him. He went a step further to say that if Thomas had known Him, he should have known His Father also; and that from that point on he knows Him, and has seen Him.

Philip, who was still having an issue with this plain truth, requested Him to show them the Father and it would suffice them. The reason for his request was because he wanted to see the Father as physically as he was seeing Jesus. Jesus then asked Philip, "Have I been with you so long, and yet you have not known Me, Philip? He who has seen Me has seen the Father; so how can you say, 'Show us the Father?' Do you not believe that I am in the Father, and the Father in Me? The words that I speak to you I do not speak on My own *authority;* but the Father who dwells in Me does the works." The Father dwells in the Son, Jesus, as the soul of man dwells in his body. This indicates that Jesus, the Son, is the Body of God, the Father.

He then asked them to believe that He is in the Father, and the Father is in Him: or else believe Him for the sake of His works (John

14:11). His demand on them to believe that the Father is in Him is because a man's physical eyes cannot see his soul, except by revelation. But because the works which the invisible Father does through the visible Son can be seen, they recommend Him to be believed. Jesus, the Son, therefore, concluded this dialogue on the need to believe also in Him.

As for Thomas, it was after Jesus had been resurrected, and, for his sake, appeared to them again that he finally believed (John 20:27). As soon as Jesus appeared, He called on him to reach hither his finger, and behold His hands; and reach hither his hand and thrust *it* into His side: and be not faithless, but believing. It was after this practical demonstration that Thomas believed that Jesus, whom he had known all the while, was the Way to the Father.

Thomas then answered in John 20:28, "My Lord and My God!" Jesus answered and said unto him, "Thomas, because you have seen Me, you have believed. Blessed *are* those who have not seen and *yet* have believed."

Many, however, have heard about Jesus but have not yet believed in Him. It is dangerous to die in the state of unbelief in Jesus. The belief of such a person in God will not save him or her from the torment in hell. Everyone that ends in hell will believe in Jesus, but it will be too late to repent then. *Whoever goes to hell after death does so from the platform of belief in God without believing also in Jesus, for He is the only way to God. It will be the outcome of tragic carelessness* [italics for emphasis).

He Is Your Life

Jesus was teaching a multitude of people on a mountain at the commencement of His ministry. On that occasion, He declared His commitment to fulfill the Law and the Prophets. He said, "Do not think that I came to destroy the Law or the Prophets, I did not come to destroy but to fulfill. For assuredly, I say to you, till heaven and earth pass away, one jot or one tittle will by no means pass from the Law till all is fulfilled" (Matthew 5:17–18). This commitment is confirmed with regard to Him being your life as Moses, in the Law, declared.

Moses, in Deuteronomy 30:19–20, warned the Israelites about the danger inherent in being drawn away to worship and serve other gods in the land that He was giving to them. Moses says, "I call heaven and earth as witnesses today against you, that I have set before you, life and death, blessing and cursing; therefore choose life, that both you and your descendants may live; that you may love the LORD your God, that you may obey His voice, and that you may cling to Him, for He is your life and the length of your days; and that you may dwell in the land which the LORD swore to your fathers, to Abraham, Isaac, and Jacob, to give them."

In that Scripture is an important statement of only four words. They are, "He *is* your life." The statement refers to the LORD your God. It conveys the truth that as you continue to love Him, obey His voice and cling to Him, you shall be having life and abundance of it.

It Is Your Life

After Moses had ended communicating the words of God to the Israelites, he then commanded them thus: "Set your hearts on all the words which I testify among you today, which you shall command your children to be careful to observe – all the words of this Law. For it is not a futile thing for you, because it is your life, and by this word you shall prolong your days in the land which you cross over the Jordan to possess" (Deuteronomy 32:46–47). In that Scripture is also an important statement of only four words. They are, "It *is* your life." The statement refers to the words of the LORD your God.

Jesus was the LORD that came to fulfill the Law and the prophets. Every word of God either in the form of law or counsel refers to Him. If "Jesus is your life," and "The word of God is also your life," then Jesus and the word of God are the same, life. This, no doubt, is responsible for John opening his gospel thus, "In the beginning was the Word, and the Word was with God, and the Word was God" (John 1:1). It is, also, no wonder, that Jesus told His audience in John 6:63, "It is the Spirit who gives life; the flesh profits nothing. The words that I speak to you are spirit, and *they* are life." He could, therefore, tell His disciples, and by extension the whole world, "I am… the life." Hence, indeed, He did not come to destroy the law and the prophets but to fulfill them.

CHAPTER 8

Jesus, the only Savior of the World

In Part I, I proved that God is not partial with three chapters. The topic of the first chapter is *God Confirms His Impartiality with Birth.* The topic of the second is *God Is No Respecter of Persons.* The third is *"...Jacob Have I Loved, but Esau Have I Hated."* But as regards getting to Him after physical or first death, God is emphatic that there is only one way to tread so as to avoid perishing or suffering the second death (John 3:16; Revelation 2:11).

He commanded Israel, saying, "You shall have no other gods before Me" (Exodus 20:3). God followed the release of the Ten Commandments with the establishment of Judaism. It became the religion of the Jews. Specifically with respect to other nations' worship of idols, God gave an additional instruction to the Israelites. They were to destroy their altars, break their images and cut down their groves (Exodus 34:13; Deuteronomy 7:5; 12:3). By giving such severe instructions, did God mean that Judaism would be a means to avoid perishing?

The message of God through Angel Gabriel to Joseph to whom the Virgin Mary was betrothed had helped to answer that question. But, for the avoidance of doubt, the LORD God did not aim that Judaism would save man from perishing. The task I am to accomplish with this chapter, therefore, is to prove by the Scripture that Jesus is the only Savior of the Jews and other nations.

The Samaritans Testified that Jesus Is the Messiah

Jesus gave nine testimonies to prove that He is one with God the Father. Before I present them, I shall first of all examine the outcome of His encounter with the Samaritans. At the end of the encounter, they believed and testified that He is the Messiah. The encounter first involved a woman after which several Samaritans came on the scene. Their meeting place was at the well of Jacob in Sychar.

The Scripture says, "But He needed to go through Samaria" (John 4:4). This is like saying that the Father had commanded Him to pass through Samaria on His homeward journey from Judea to Galilee. This was despite the strained relationship that existed between the Jews and the Samaritans at the time.

Jesus was wearied by this journey. Therefore, He and His disciples stopped at this well to rest a while. All the disciples then went to town to buy food. While they were away, the woman came to draw water. The time was about noon. Jesus requested of her water to drink. She, however, was not willing to grant His request. She gave two reasons for refusing. The first arose from the subsisting strained relationship between the two nations. She, therefore, asked the Lord Jesus how it was that He being a Jew asked her, a Samaritan, for water.

Jesus said to her, "If you knew the gift of God, and who it is who says to you, 'Give Me to drink,' you would have asked Him, and He would have given you living water" (John 4:10). Jesus is the gift of God to the world (John 3:16). A key word in His answer is the verb "knew." Jesus had embarked on this journey so that the Samaritans might get to know the gift of God and who personifies it. The journey was like a familiarization tour. Jesus already knew the Samaritans. This is because, being Omniscient, He knows all people (John 3:24). He also knows what was, is, and will be in any person (John 3:25).

But the Samaritans needed to know Him. By knowing Him, they could then get to know the invisible or unknown God through Him. Hence He passed by their city. But what is the importance of knowing God? The answer is given in John 17:3. The text says, "And this is eternal life, that they might know You, the only true God, and Jesus Christ, whom You have sent." A person acquires eternal life through knowing God and Jesus Christ whom He sent to the world.

Jesus' reply caused her to ask Him two questions. The first is, "... You have nothing to draw with, and the well is deep. Where then do You get that living water?" The second is, "Are You greater than our father Jacob, who gave us the well, and drank from *it* himself, as well as his sons and his livestock?"

Jesus chose not to comment about her comparison of Him with father Jacob. He refused to be drawn into the trap of comparing Himself with someone else, whoever the person may be. Those who do such, according to the Scripture, are not wise (2 Corinthians 10:12). But, Jesus, the wisdom of God (1 Corinthians 1:30), will avoid a foolish action by all means.

In the first three verses of John Chapter 4 in which the story of the woman of Samaria is told, a form of comparison has been suggested. The three verses say, "Therefore, when the Lord knew that the Pharisees had heard that Jesus made and baptized more disciples than John (though Jesus Himself did not baptize, but His disciples), He left Judea and departed again to Galilee." The section above in parenthesis implies that Jesus cannot be compared with any other human being, including John, even in the matter of baptism. John baptized people with "ordinary water," while Jesus will baptize people with "living water," which is the Holy Spirit (John 1:33; Acts 1:5).

But, back to the woman of Samaria, Jesus simply raised her expectation. This He did by telling her, "Whoever drinks of this water will thirst again, but whoever drinks of the water that I shall give him shall never thirst. But the water that I shall give him will become in him a fountain of water (which is) springing up into everlasting life" (John 4:13–14). The living water that Jesus promised her does not need to be drawn. Instead, it will be coming forth from her belly by itself.

She then responded by requesting Him to give her the water so that she does not thirst, neither come there to draw again. Jesus then directed her to go and call her husband. She declared that she had no husband. Jesus commended her for being honest. He then said, "You have well said, 'I have no husband,' for you have had five husbands, and the one whom you now have is not your husband; in that you spoke truly" (John 4:17–18).

At this point, she upgraded Him to being a Prophet. She then stated the second excuse why she should have no dealing with a Jew like Him. It was because their fathers worshipped on one specific mountain, but the Jews say that in Jerusalem is the place where men ought to worship (John 4:20). The Jews worshipped God on Mount Zion in Jerusalem. The Samaritans, on the other hand, worshipped God on Mount Gerizim. Other nations of the world, of course, also had their "mountains" on which they worshipped God. This was how she introduced religion into the dialogue.

There are about 4,300 religions, including Judaism and Christianity, in all the nations of the world, according to the record of Google. The adherents of each of them worship a Deity generally called God.

"...We Know what We Worship..."

In His response, Jesus said unto her, "Woman, believe Me, the hour is coming when you will neither on this mountain, nor in Jerusalem, worship the Father" (John 4:21). Jesus implied that the worship of the Father in a place, like a mountain, will eventually be phased out. This was one of the prophecies that Jesus came to fulfill. The specific prophecy was declared in Jeremiah 3:23. The text says, "Truly, in vain *is salvation hoped for* from the hills, *and from* the multitude of mountains; truly, in the LORD our God *is* the salvation of Israel."

Jesus, the Savior, was "the LORD our God" who was dialoguing with her. This showed the willingness of Jesus to extend that salvation to other nations of the earth. It is no wonder that after He resurrected, just before He ascended back to heaven, He mandated His disciples to be witnesses to Him beyond Samaria and to the end of the earth

(Acts 1:8). The news of the promised salvation is not to be limited to Jerusalem and Judea.

There are three fundamental reasons why worship on the mountain would be phased out ultimately. The first reason is because, "You worship what you do not know…" (John 4:22). The Samaritans do not know what or who they are worshipping. This is because God whom they claim to be worshipping is invisible to the human eyes. The second is that they had not yet known the Son, Jesus, through whom they should be worshiping God. The third is that they do not yet know how to worship Him. This is much more so because, according to Apostle Paul, "He *(God)* does not dwell in temples made with hands" (Acts 17:24). This trip was thus purposely arranged so as to address these fundamental reasons.

Jesus then went on to say, "…we *(the Jews)* know what we worship, for salvation is of the Jews" (John 4:22). This means that the Jews know about salvation and who the Savior is. This is because as the Savior of the world, He came through them by birth. Angel Gabriel told Joseph, the betrothed of the Virgin Mary, "And she shall bring forth a Son, and you shall call His name JESUS, for He will save His people from their sins" (Matthew 1:21). God promised an aged man, Simeon, that he would not see death before he had seen the Lord's Christ (Luke 2:26).

Forty days after the birth of Jesus, His mother came to the temple for her purification, and His dedication. The just and devout Simeon handled both customs of the law for the two of them. And particularly for Jesus, Simeon took Him in his hand, blessed God, and said, "Lord, now You are letting Your servant depart in peace, according to Your word; for my eyes have seen Your salvation which You have prepared before the face of all peoples, a light to *bring* revelation to the Gentiles, and the glory of Your people Israel" (Luke 2:29–32). The Jews thus knew about salvation and who the Savior is.

Meanwhile, Jesus defined who God is and how to worship Him. He said, "God *is* a Spirit: and those who worship Him must worship in spirit and truth" (John 4:24). The woman responded to the definition thus, "I know that Messiah is coming, (who is called Christ). When He comes, He will tell us all things" (John 4:25). Her statement meant that the Messiah, the Christ, when He comes, will tell them who God is, and how to worship Him.

This was when Jesus was literally compelled to reveal His identity to her. He said, "I who speak to you am *He*" (John 4:26). Jesus' statement means that "I am the Messiah, the Christ, who was to come." He thus presented Himself to this strange Samaritan woman as the Savior of the world. It is only Jesus Christ, the Son of God, also known as Emmanuel, that can save. No religion can.

This presentation tallies with what Jesus told His disciples in the Upper Room following the request of Thomas who had asked Him, "Lord, we do not know where You are going, and how can we know the way?" "Jesus said unto him, 'I am the way, and the truth, and the life: no man comes to the Father except through Me. If you had known Me, you would have known My Father also; and from now on you know Him, and have *seen* Him'" (John 14:6–7).

That statement of Jesus suggests that the Father is exactly like Him. This suggestion is correct because Jesus is "the Godhead Bodily" (the Body of God) (Colossians 2:8–9), even as the Father is "the Godhead" (the Soul of God) (Acts 17:28–31). This is such as the soul of a man is as his body. Hence, the visible Jesus is one with the invisible Father (John 10:30). This is also as the visible soil in the dust of the ground is one with the invisible seed in the same dust of the ground. They are one because they are trapped together, although loosely.

A True Worshipper of God

Jesus earlier said to her, "But the hour is coming, and now is, when the true worshippers will worship the Father in spirit and truth; for the Father is seeking such to worship Him" (John 4:23). The hour that would soon come was the time of His crucifixion. He would then qualify to be revealed through His resurrection to be the Savior of the world.

Before I proceed with the dialogue between Jesus and this woman, I shall shed some light on who is a true worshipper. The adjective "true" which qualifies the noun "worshipper" shows that heaven is the theater of activity. Two Scriptures confirm that the location is heaven. They are John 6:32 and Hebrews 8:1–2. The first text refers to Jesus as "the true bread from heaven." The second also refers to heaven being where the throne of Jesus is located. The location is described as the true tabernacle which the Lord pitched and not man. Jesus is also described as a Minister in that true tabernacle.

Furthermore, Jesus in John 15:1 describes Himself as the True Vine, and His Father as the Husbandman. This is another proof of heaven being the location that Jesus refers to. Therefore, the branches referred to in John 15:2 are none other than the angels. One of them was Lucifer who eventually went into perdition (Isaiah 14:12–15). As against being the True Vine in heaven, on earth, He is the Vine and His human disciples are His branches (John 15:5). Lucifer, the branch of the True Vine, was cast out from heaven. In like manner, Judas Iscariot, the branch of the Vine, was cast into perdition from the earth.

Man is not a spirit but a living soul. Man cannot, therefore, give worship in spirit that he is not. God comes in to help him by giving him His words which are spirit and life. This necessitates the exercise of understanding, knowledge, and wisdom of God. In addition, by the nature inherited from Adam, man is a liar. The Scripture says, "The wicked are estranged from the womb; they go astray as soon as they are born, speaking lies" (Psalm 58:3). So, like Satan, the prince of the world, there is no truth in man (John 8:44). Man cannot, therefore, worship God in truth.

Therefore, each person must first of all be made a spirit before becoming a true worshipper of God in spirit and truth. And this can only be after his death. His dead body shall also have been resurrected from the grave and merged with his soul which had hitherto been in heaven. This is how he becomes a spirit like God. It is then that such a person will be able to worship God in spirit and truth. This is how a man can be a true worshipper of God.

The "Food of Jesus" and the "Will of God"

To continue where I left off, the disciples returned with food at the point when Jesus disclosed His identity to the woman. They marveled that He talked with her. None of them, however, asked her what she was seeking? And none also asked Jesus why He was talking with her. The woman then abandoned her pot at the well, and went back to town. What she was going to town for they could not tell, but Jesus must have known.

Meanwhile, she went to tell the news in town of a man who told her everything she ever did. She had asked them, "Is this not the Christ?" The Samaritans responded by coming enmass with her to meet with Jesus.

But before she came back with the crowd, the disciples tried to persuade Him to eat, but He was not disposed to. He said to them, "I have meat to eat that you know not of." They wondered if anybody had brought Him food to eat. Jesus then said, "My food is to do the will of Him who sent Me, and to finish his work…" (John 4:34–38). The "food of Jesus" and the "will of God" are to save the world, for that was the purpose for His birth. Jesus thus claims to be the only Savior of the world.

A Word of Knowledge, Belief, Testimony, Teaching or Preaching the Word

Four sequential actions are presented by this episode to accomplish the great task of saving the world. First, what Jesus revealed about her movement from one man to another constituted a word of knowledge. Second, the truth of the word of knowledge convinced her to believe that Jesus is the Messiah. Third, the woman used what Jesus revealed about her as a testimony to draw a crowd of people to Him. Four, Jesus used the word of God in the form of teaching and preaching to cause the Samaritans to believe in Him.

They believed in Jesus to be the Savior. They were so convinced about who He is that they persuaded Him to tarry with them. He abode there two days. Many more believed because of His word. They knew that He is indeed the Christ, the Savior of the world.

A Prophet Is not Without Honor

The needed conviction that Jesus is the only Savior is at the very foundation of the concept of the Trinity of God. But the Jews and, indeed, much of the whole world have a very serious issue with this concept. Failure to embrace it and then understand it will debar any reader of the Bible the necessary understanding. This was a major reason why the Pharisees that Jesus once dialogued with alleged that He was mad and wondered why some people were listening to Him.

The LORD says in Isaiah 65:1, "…I was found by *those who* did not seek Me…." The Samaritans did not seek Jesus, the Savior, yet they found Him and believed in Him. But the Jews that sought Him, and to whom He came, because of their failure to believe in Him, did not find Him. And this is because a prophet is not without honor save in his own country, and in his own house (Matthew 13:57; Mark 6:4; Luke 4:24; John 4:44). A word of knowledge which Jesus gave was the means by which several Samaritans believed in Him to be the Messiah, Christ, the Savior.

The Prophet like Moses whom the LORD God promised to send to Israel eventually appeared as Jesus. He was going about doing good works. He healed a man that had suffered paralysis for thirty-eight years at the Pool of Bethesda. He did the miracle in Jerusalem on a Sabbath day. This miracle should have equally caused the Jews to believe in Him to be the Messiah. Rather than do, the leaders of the Jews became determined by it to kill Him.

The Samaritans did not seek Jesus, the Savior, yet they found Him and believed in Him. But the Jews that sought Him, and to whom He came, because of their failure to believe in Him, did not find Him.

The first reason for wanting to kill Him was for supposedly working on a Sabbath day. The second was for telling the man to "rise, take up your bed and walk." They interpreted the instruction to the man as authorizing him to violate the law of a Sabbath day. Jesus told them point blank: "My Father has been working until now, and I have been working" (John 5:17). This claim further enraged those leaders. They, therefore, sought to kill Him for a third reason. This was for calling Himself the Son of God. This is a title which they rightly equated with being equal with God.

At this stage, Jesus decided to testify about His Sonship of God and oneness with the Father. He would thereby prove that He is the only way to the Father, which is the same as being the only Savior.

The First Testimony of Jesus by Himself

The first testimony of Jesus is stated in John 5:19. The text says, "Most assuredly, I say to you, the Son can do nothing of Himself, but what

He sees the Father do; for whatever He does, the Son also does in like manner."

The body of a man is one with his soul. The soil and the seed in the dust of the ground are regarded as one. This is because the seed in the dust of the ground is invisible to the human eyes. Therefore, man cannot separate it from the soil. The seed and the soil are thus one. They are literally joined together, though loosely.

When God formed man with them, the soil became the body and the seed became the soul. And because man is the image of God, Jesus, the Son of God, who can be seen, represents the Body of God. God the Father, who cannot be seen, represents the Soul of God. And if Jesus sees what the Father does before doing the same thing, then He must have seen the Father also.

This testimony presents Jesus, first, to be like the body of a man. The body of a man cannot do anything by itself but what his soul does. And because the body of a man is one with his soul, Jesus thus claims by this testimony to be one with God.

Second, the oneness of Jesus and the Father is of a much higher level than that of a man's body and his soul. This is because a man's eyes cannot see his soul except momentarily by revelation, whereas, according to John 5:19, Jesus sees the Father always. This point implies that the two of them are individually identifiable. Jesus had confirmed this difference in identity by our key text of John 14:1. It says, "...You believe in God, believe also in Me." Two different Persons, one called the Father, and the other, the Son. The first one, the Father, has been believed; and the other, Jesus, is also to be believed.

In effect, if someone does not believe the two Personalities, his or her belief cannot achieve the purpose intended. Hence, they are one as Jesus said, even though the people took offense. Furthermore, if the body fails to physically carry out what the soul does, the outcome of the work of the body will turn out to be a visible mistake or failure. I shall explain this point with an example. It is that of two gates.

Suppose there are two gates having two different padlocks with each padlock having its different key. The correct keys would be needed to open each of the two padlocks. Let us suppose that the soul is set on opening the second padlock so as to gain access into the second room. The key that opens the padlock of the door of the second room would be needed. But if the key of the first padlock is taken and used, it will not serve the intended purpose. The action will turn out to be a mistake. Consequently, there can be no entry into the desired room. This shows that the soul of a man is the director of the body. The body of man needs to be coordinated with it through the mind. This way, mistake can be avoided.

This was how Jesus went about His mission to the earth without making any mistake. As the body of God, He strictly followed the directive of the Father, the Soul of God, in every of His assignments. And this was possible for Him because He could see God. And this is because they are one. Hence they could be in contact with each other everywhere and every time.

The Second Testimony of Jesus by Himself

The second testimony of Jesus is recorded in John 5:20. It goes thus, "For the Father loves the Son, and shows Him *all* (italics for emphasis) things that He Himself does; and he will show Him greater works than these, that you may marvel."

The Father loves Jesus. Jesus also notes that the Father loves the disciples as He has loved Him. He confirms this in His final prayer in John 17:23. He says: "I in them, and You in Me; that they may be made perfect in one, and that the world may know that You have sent Me, and have loved them, as You have loved Me." So, Jesus is not the only person that the Father loves. He (the Father) loved the world, and gave His Son whom He loves to it. What an expansive environment of love we dwell in!

No human being can see God and not die. Even Moses who was highly esteemed by God and the Jews could not see the face of God and live. Moses requested to see the glory of God. But God told him "You cannot see My face; for no man shall see Me, and live" (Exodus 33:20). Only Jesus, the Spirit, and both good and evil angels enjoyed the privilege of seeing God. And this privilege is much more so for Jesus when He was here on earth as the Son of God and the Son of Man. And if the pure in heart can see God (Matthew 5:8), Jesus' ability to see God when He was on earth confirms that He possessed a pure heart.

What is the significance of Moses not being able to see the face of God? First, it suggests that as meek as he was, yet his heart was not pure enough to see God. Second, it is after death that any man can hope to see the face of God. And that will depend upon such a man's body being qualified to be resurrected unto eternal life. Therefore, for a man, like Moses, to request to see God is a desire to die. This will not be profitable for him. But by Jesus seeing God the Father and yet remain alive shows that He was a special Man with a pure heart. He was the special Son of God who was conceived in a special way. He could, therefore, see the invisible God and not die.

John the Baptist by the Spirit in John 3:27 says, "A man can receive nothing unless it has been given to him from heaven." The Father was showing Jesus all the things that He was doing. Jesus was ever ready to do them the way the Father was doing them. Therefore, nothing could hinder the successful implementation of the things being done. This second point again affirms the oneness of the two of them, with both also having the same program. They are absolutely in agreement.

Before I sign off this second testimony, I shall consider one more point. A part of what Jesus said is that the Father shows Him all things that He does. This means that at every point in time when the Father does anything, He shows it to the Son. Can an earthly father show his son *all* [italics for emphasis] things that he does and at every time? Even if the father tries to, can the son see all he does, especially when they are not always in the same place? The correct answer is, "No".

Therefore, the implications of the Father showing all things that He does to Jesus are two-fold. First, it shows that the type of relationship that exists between God the Father and His Son, Jesus Christ, far surpasses that between a man and his son. Second, it shows that an earthly son is not one with his father like Jesus, the Son of God, is, with His Father. Therefore, the use of the phrase, "Son of God," is meant to describe, in human sense, the very close relationship that exists between God the Father and Jesus.

The Third Testimony of Jesus by Himself

The third testimony of Jesus says, "For as the Father raises the dead and gives life to *them,* even so the Son gives life to whom He will" (John 5:21).

This Scripture presents two types of quickening which the New King James' Version translates as "gives life to." The first is that which is by the Father. He raises the dead and quickens them. The second is the one by the Son. He quickens whom He wills. There are three examples of dead people that Jesus brought back to life during His earthly ministry. The three examples will help us to understand the two types of quickening.

The raising of the son of the widow of Nain is Number 1 (Luke 7:11–15). Jesus was going into the city. Right at the city gate, He was met by a funeral cortège. This incident presented an example of divine timing, for, according to Larry Huch, "In the ancient Hebrew language, there is no word for coincidence."[7] So, it was not coincidental

[7] Larry Huch: *4 Blood Moons: Your Future Begins Now*, page 11 [Published by Winter Publishing LLC 2448 E. 81st St. Suite #4802, Tulsa Oklahoma 74137 USA.]

that Jesus met the grieving mother. He saw it coming and moved to reverse the terrible incidence. It was the only son of a widow that was being carried out of the city to be buried. The mother was in tears. She was going to witness the burial of her only son as she did that of her husband. Naturally, Jesus had compassion on her. He interrupted the cortège. He first consoled the mourning mother by telling her, "Weep not." He then proceeded to touch the coffin. He said, "Young man, I say unto you, 'Arise.'" He that had died sat up, and began to speak. The mother joyfully received her son back alive.

The raising of the daughter of Jairus, a ruler of the synagogue, is Number 2 (Matthew 9:18–19, 23–26; Mark 5:22–23, 35–43). Jairus had requested Jesus to come and touch his daughter who was dying. Before He got to her, she had died. Some of the mourners came to tell Jairus not to bother Jesus any longer because the damsel had died. Jesus heard the sad news. He quickly told him not to be afraid, but only believe.

When He finally got to the ruler's house, He put away everybody and entered into where she was laid. In the company of her mother, father, three of His disciples, and the damsel, they were altogether seven people in the room. He simply said *Talitha cumin*. This is interpreted to mean, "Damsel, I say unto you, 'Arise.'" The damsel arose and was given food to eat.

The Number 3 example, which was the quickening of Lazarus (John 11:40–44), was not the same as the two earlier examples. In the example of Lazarus, Jesus gave the glory to God from whom it was derived. This was why He asked Martha, "Did I not say to you that if you would believe you would see the glory of God?"

At the side of the grave, Jesus lifted up His eyes, and said, "Father, I thank You that You have heard Me. And I know that You always hear Me, but because of the people who are standing by I said *this*, that they may believe that You sent Me." The man had died and his body had been buried for four days. His body had decayed. Actually, Martha said that he already was stinking. He, however, cried with a loud voice, "Lazarus, come forth." Jesus raised and quickened Lazarus and ordered them to "loose him, and let him go."

The first two examples show that Jesus acted as God. He acted without reference to God the Father on the basis of either compassion for, or belief of, the bereaved. On the basis of the third example, it shows that Jesus can act jointly with God the Father. And this is meant for the glory of God the Father and to glorify Jesus whom He sent to the world.

But most importantly, the segment of the pronouncement of Jesus which says, "That they may believe that You had sent Me" is a direct reference to the plan of the LORD God to raise up unto them a Prophet from the midst of them, "of your brethren." The Prophet shall be from the midst of them. He shall also be of their brethren. He would be like Moses. Unto Him they shall hearken. He would put His words in His mouth. He shall speak unto them all that He, the LORD God, shall command Him. But whosoever will not hearken unto the words of the LORD God which He shall speak in His name, it will be required of him (Deuteronomy 18:1–2).

Jesus was thus stating in unequivocal terms that He is that Prophet that Moses prophesied about. Hence, He had earlier said in John 5:46–47, "If you believed Moses, you would believe Me; for he wrote about Me. But if you do not believe his writings, how will you believe My words?"

The Fourth Testimony of Jesus by Himself

The fourth testimony of Jesus says, "For the Father judges no one, but has committed all judgment to the Son" (John 5:22). What is the role of a judge? According to Google, a judge who determines guilt in criminal cases may impose a sentence or penalty on the guilty party.

In civil cases, the judge may award relief, such as compensation for damages to the parties who win the lawsuit.

A sentence or penalty can be in the form of imprisonment for a period. Jesus as a judge can punish a person with imprisonment in hell or reward a person with a mansion in heaven. Should a reasonable person not seek the love of such a person? Should a person not behave well before such a person?

The Fifth Testimony of Jesus by Himself

The fifth testimony of Jesus says, "That all should honor the Son just as they honor the Father. He who does not honor the Son does not honor the Father who sent Him" (John 5:23).

This testimony is closely tied to the third and fourth. This is because it is wise to honor a person that has such a tremendous power of life and death. This is even more so because one cannot see the Father to honor. This is like saying that the only opportunity one has to honor the Father is by honoring the Son. This is because He is the God that anybody can see and relate with physically. Nobody can relate with someone he cannot see physically. Refusal to honor the Son, who can be seen, therefore, is tantamount to rejecting the only means man has to honor God the Father. And if transgressing the command of God to honor a human father earns one physical death (Matthew 15:4), refusal to honor God the Father would earn one eternal death.

The story of King Herod would help us to understand this testimony of Jesus. This was the Herod that killed James the son of Zebedee, one of the disciples of Jesus, the brother of John. When he saw that the Jews were pleased with his action, he again arrested Peter and locked him up in prison. He waited for an opportune time to kill him also. The Church, however, prayed and Peter was miraculously released from prison. The release of Peter did not go down well with Herod who was naturally annoyed with the security officers. When he could not find Peter, he killed the security personnel. He took several lives in place of Peter's.

King Herod was also annoyed with the people of Tyre and Sidon. On a set day, they came in order to appease him. When he addressed the people publicly, they praised him by calling him god and not man. He received the honor. One could imagine him nodding his head forward and backward as acceptance of the honor which he did not deserve. Instantly, an angel of the LORD struck him dead. He was eaten up by worms (Acts 12:19–23). But this was not so with Jesus.

Whoever is honoring Jesus is directly honoring God. Jesus cannot, therefore, incur God's wrath as Herod did. Those who claim to honor the Father but fail to honor the Son are not being truthful. This is because, according to 1 John 4:20, whoever does not honor the Son of God whom he can see, how can he claim to honor God whom he cannot see?

The Sixth Testimony of Jesus by Himself

The sixth testimony of Jesus goes thus, "Most assuredly, I say to you, 'He who hears My word and believes in Him who sent Me has everlasting life, and shall not come into judgment, but has passed from death into life'" (John 5:24).

Jesus implies by His statement that the way a man can show that he believes in God that cannot be seen is to believe that the word He, Jesus, speaks is the word of the Father who sent Him. This is the way to escape condemnation, and to pass from death into life. What a simple way this is to enjoy eternal life!

This testimony serves those who did not see Jesus physically when He was on earth. They neither saw the Father nor His Son. But they lose nothing, provided they believe the written word

Those who claim to honor the Father but fail to honor the Son are not being truthful.

of Jesus to be the word of God. They, too, shall escape condemnation, and pass from death unto life.

The Seventh Testimony of Jesus by Himself

The seventh testimony of Jesus goes thus, "Most assuredly, I say to you, the hour is coming, and now is, when the dead will hear the voice of the Son of God; and those who hear will live" (John 5:25).

Since the creation and formation of man, because of the sin of disobedience of the first Adam, people had been dying. The bodies of such people were and are being buried or cremated. Jesus means by His statement above that it was not over with such bodies. He means that a time is coming, and that it is even now, when such dead, buried or cremated bodies, will hear His voice. The time that is "even now" refers to His crucifixion, burial, and resurrection. What one should seriously ponder on is the last segment of the testimony. It says, "...and those who hear will live." This makes Him the Resurrection and the Life (John 11:25).

The Eighth Testimony of Jesus by Himself

The eighth testimony of Jesus immediately follows the six words "... and those who hear will live." The text of the eighth testimony says, "For as the Father has life in Himself, so He has granted the Son to have life in Himself, and has given Him authority to execute judgment also, because He is the Son of Man. Do not marvel at this; for the hour is coming in which all who are in the graves will hear His voice and shall come forth–those who have done good, to the resurrection of life, and those who have done evil, to the resurrection of condemnation" (John 5: 26–29).

The Father had given Jesus to have life and has given Him authority to execute judgment. Jesus has, consequently, decreed the condition for giving the dead bodies of people life. The condition precedent, for the sake of emphasis, is to hear His voice. It is His voice which utters

God's word that they shall live by. When Jesus resurrected, the bodies of several dead and buried people were raised up from the graves. Of course, the respective souls of such saints which had been in paradise merged with their resurrected bodies. It is all who are in the graves that will hear His voice and shall come forth.

The phrase "all who are in the graves" means that both saints and sinners will hear His voice and come forth. But it is where the bodies go to after they resurrect that is of paramount importance. The saints among them resurrected and merged with their respective souls and went with Jesus to heaven. Several of such saints were seen in the city. Matthew 27:52–53 captures the event thus, "And the graves were opened; and many bodies of the saints who had fallen asleep were raised; and coming out of the graves after His resurrection, they went into the holy city and appeared to many." A person like one of the malefactors that was crucified by His side was privileged to hear His voice. He had, earlier, heard Him say to him, "Assuredly, I say to you, today you will be with Me in paradise" (Luke 23:43).

I presume that the graves of sinners were also opened. And the bodies of these ones that failed to believe in Jesus were also resurrected. A person like the other malefactor that was crucified by the side of Jesus must have failed to hear His voice. As a matter of fact, Jesus did not address him. His buried body was, however, also resurrected on the third day. It would, therefore, have merged with his soul and continued to suffer intensely in hell.

The Ninth Testimony of Jesus by Himself

The ninth testimony of Jesus as documented in John 5:30 says, "I can of Myself do nothing. As I hear, I judge: and My judgment is righteous, because I do not seek My own will but the will of the Father who sent Me."

There is constant communication between the soul of man and his body. The communication is to and fro. What the body hears from the soul is what it does. This means that before you suddenly stand up and move from one spot to another, there had been a communication between your soul and the body. The soul had silently told the body what to do and it had obeyed by moving through the senses in the body. This is what also takes place between God the Father, the Soul of God, and His Son Jesus Christ, the Body of God.

He confirms this to-and-fro communication between Him and the Father with how judgment is delivered. When He sets to deliver judgment, even though it had been committed to Him, it is what the Father communicates to Him that He pronounces as judgment (John 5:22, 27, 30). The Son does not have a minority judgment on any matter. He is strictly bound by the will of the Father. This is what Jesus identifies as being given commandment by the Father. He declared, "For I have not spoken on My own *authority*; but the Father who sent Me gave Me a command, what I should say and what I should speak" (John 12:49). And He strictly obeys, hence He said, "And I know that His command is everlasting life. Therefore, whatever I speak, just as the Father has told Me, so I speak" (John 12:50).

This does not imply an instruction by a superior to a subordinate. Instead, it is communication from one member of a group to another, each occupying His unique position. This is so because they are one as body and soul of man are. This shows how Jesus demonstrated unparalleled humility by accepting to be sent to the world as a servant. This unique attribute of humility is what Apostle Paul addresses in Philippians 2:5–11: "Let this mind be in you which was also in Christ Jesus, who, being in the form of God, did not consider it robbery to be equal with God, but made Himself of no reputation, taking the form of a bondservant, and coming in the likeness of men. And being found in appearance as a man, He humbled Himself and became obedient to *the point of* death, even the death of the cross. Therefore God also has highly exalted Him and given Him the name which is above every name, that at the name of Jesus every knee should bow, of those in heaven, and of those on earth, and of those under the earth, and that every tongue should confess that Jesus Christ *is* Lord, to the glory of God the Father."

In the light of the foregoing explanations, I hereby conclude this chapter thus: Jesus is God. He is one with God the Father. He is the Son of God. He is the promised Prophet. He is the only Way to the Father. He is the Savior of the world. These are what the concept of God's Trinity makes clear about Him. It is, therefore, dangerous not to take what He says serious, and act on them.

CHAPTER 9

The Work of God Is to Believe that Jesus Is God

Free Supply of Food

Jesus had fed about 5,000 people in the wilderness with only five loaves of bread and two pieces of fish. This figure does not include women and children. After this free supply of food, the people He fed said, "This is truly the Prophet who is to come into the world" (John 6:14). This is the closest that the Jews came to recognizing Him as a prophet like Moses that God promised to send (Deuteronomy 18:18–19). But their recognition of Him was for an entirely different reason. It wasn't for salvation from sin, but constant supply of free food.

Jesus perceived that they would come and take Him by force to make Him a king (John 6:15). They wanted Him to become their "Father Christmas." This would amount to a diversion of the purpose of His mission to the world. Therefore, He went away from the region where He had fed the crowd. But they would not give up their search for Him.

They eventually found Him on the other side of the Sea of Galilee. They then asked Him, "Rabbi, when did You come here?" Jesus knew their motive for coming to Him. He, therefore, said to them, "Most assuredly, I say to you, you seek Me, not because you saw the signs, but because you ate of the loaves and were filled. Do not labor for the food which perishes, but for the food which endures to everlasting life, which the Son of Man will give you, because God the Father has set His seal on Him" (John 6:25–27). In response to this important information, they asked Him, "What shall we do, that we may work the works of God?" Jesus answered, "This is the work of God, that you believe in Him whom He sent" (John 6:29).

The Truth Is that Jesus Is God

Jesus was going about teaching people. He was preaching the gospel of the Kingdom of God to them and performing miracles. This was how He was showing compassion. One of the purposes of these activities was for His disciples and the generality of the Jews to believe that He was sent by the Father. Many of them, indeed, believed in Him as a result of these activities. He then told them to continue in His word, and that it is then that they are His disciples, indeed. The result of their positive response would be that they shall know the truth, and it shall make them free (John 8:30–32).

Multitudes of people, however, have an issue with Jesus being regarded as God. An example was my cousin who totally refused to believe that Jesus is God. He stated his reason for not believing that Jesus is God in the form of a question. He asked me, "How can someone who is sent be of the same status with the one who sent him?" He, thus, concluded that Jesus is not God!

His view seems to be supported by what Jesus says in John 17:3. In that text, Jesus says, "And this is life eternal, that they might know You, the only true God, and Jesus Christ, whom You have sent." In that text, Jesus introduces God the Father as "the only true God." He also introduces Himself, firstly, as Christ, and secondly, as someone who is sent. Does He, thereby, exclude Himself from being God by introducing the Father as the only true God? And does He mean that He is not God because God sent Him?

The Proof that Jesus Is God

I shall prove that Jesus is God even though He introduced the Father as the only true God. His status as God, despite His claim of being sent, is not diminished either. The text of John 17:3 is a unique one. It is unique in that it shows how God hides Himself. The practice of God hiding Himself is documented in Isaiah 45:15. That Scripture says, "Truly You *are* God, who hide Yourself, O God of Israel, the Savior." The New International Version (NIV) translates that text thus: Truly You are a God who hides Himself, O God and Savior of Israel."

Jesus claimed that He was sent to the world in this unique text as the Christ. The title "Christ" means "the anointed One." This claim was confirmed by the revelation of God the Father to Peter. Jesus had asked His disciples, "…who do you say that I am?" Peter answered and said, "You are the Christ, the Son of the Living God" (Matthew 16:16). Jesus answered and said to him, "Blessed are you, Simon Bar-Jonah, for flesh and blood has not revealed *this* to you, but My Father who is in heaven" (Matthew 18:17). Faith is required to accept that Jesus is God as per God's revelation to Peter.

Anybody can, however, be anointed. God sent Prophet Samuel to anoint Saul, the son of Kish, a Benjamite (1 Samuel 10:1). He also sent him to anoint David, the son of Jesse, a Bethlehemite (1 Samuel 16:13). They were both anointed on two different occasions to make them kings. Their anointing did not make any of them God. It may, therefore, not be readily accepted, because of anointing, that Jesus is God.

Jesus' personal declaration of His anointing, which is documented in Luke 4:18–19, also requires faith to accept. The text says, "The Spirit of the LORD *is* upon Me, because He has anointed Me to preach the gospel to the poor; He has sent Me to heal the broken-hearted, to proclaim liberty to *the* captives and recovery of sight to *the* blind, to set at liberty those who are oppressed; to proclaim the acceptable year of the LORD." The people of Nazareth, His hometown, however, refused to accept His testimony.

The custodians of the Scripture, namely, the priests, scribes, Sadducees, and Pharisees did worse. They were the ones that saw to it that He was crucified for claiming to be the Son of God. It is, also, not everybody that God sent to the world that is God. For example, God sent many prophets, such as Moses, Elijah, Elisha, Isaiah to the world, but that did not make them God. The person that came closest to being God was Moses, who was made a god to Pharaoh (Exodus 7:1).

Therefore, it requires practical and convincing proof, apart from miracles, that Jesus was, indeed, sent as God. And to do this, I will need to go back to the beginning of the story of creation.

The Name of the First Object Used to Form Man Is Mentioned

The first object that was mentioned in the list of what God used to form man is the dust of the ground. The text of Genesis 2:7 says, "And the LORD God formed man of the dust of the ground, and breathed into his nostrils the breath of life; and man became a living soul." The visible and inorganic soil in the dust of the ground, which is made up of elements such as calcium, potassium, iron, carbon, zinc, gasses, water, etc., became the visible body of man.

The Name of the Second Object Used to Form Man Is Not Mentioned

God did not mention the name of the second object in the dust of the ground in the list of what He used to form man. He had, however, already deposited it in the dust of the ground at the time He created the earth on the third day. He made reference to it again on the sixth day. He was more specific about it in Genesis 1:29a. The text says, "And God said, 'See, I have given you every herb *that* yields seed which *is* on the face of all the earth....'"

This seed that every herb yields, and which is on the face of all the earth, is invisible to the human eyes and is organic. This is where God hides the truth about the trinity of man. This truth naturally sheds some light on His own Trinity since He created man in His image and likeness. It is this invisible seed, which is organic, that became a living invisible soul of man after God breathed the breath of life into the nostrils of man that He formed with the dust of the ground. And since man is the image of God, therefore, the invisible God is the Soul of God.

The Name of the Third Object Used to Form Man Is Mentioned

The third and last, but not the least thing, in the list of what God used to form man, was His breath. God's breath which He breathed into the nostrils of the man became his spirit. It activated the man. It enables the three parts of man, namely, body, soul, and spirit (1 Thessalonians 5:23) to dwell together on the earth.

The Trinity and Sabbath of Rest

From the foregoing, it is clear that the earth supplies two components, soil and seed, with which the trinity of man was formed. What is that thing that can be added to those two components to form *the trinity of the earth* as God added His breath, which became man's spirit? This question can be paraphrased through three consecutive steps. The first step is that the body of man is like the soil in the earth. The second step is that the soul of man is like the invisible seed in the earth. The third step is the paraphrased question. It is this: "What can the spirit of man be likened to with reference to the earth, which will directly affect both the soil and the seed?"

The answer to that question can be found in the inspired statement of Apostle Paul in Galatians 6:8. The text says, "For he that sows to his flesh shall of the flesh reap corruption; but he that sows to the spirit shall of the spirit reap life eternal." Therefore, the spirit of man can be likened to sowing seed in the soil of the earth. The trinity of the earth is, thus, namely, soil, seed, and sowing.

The earth that does not bring forth herb, grass, and tree is assumed to be barren. In the alternative, it is assumed to be fertile when the seed sown in it brings forth fruit. This enjoins us to sow to spiritual things so as to reap eternal life. Hence, he who sows sparingly, therefore, shall reap sparingly; and he who sows bountifully shall reap also bountifully (2 Corinthians 9:6). And to show that sowing is a spiritual step, Apostle Paul again says, "I have planted, Apollos watered; but God gave the increase. So then neither is he that plants anything, neither he that waters; but God that gives the increase" (1 Corinthians 3:6–7). This shows the involvement of the Spirit *(God)* as far as the trinity of the earth is concerned.

The Scripture in Genesis 2:3 says, "And God blessed the seventh day, and sanctified it: because that in it He had rested from all His work which God created and made." The emphasis that God placed on the seventh day, to the extent of sanctifying it, and also calling it by a special name, sabbath, was because it was the day He rested. After God created and formed man in His image as trinity, He commanded him to also rest on the seventh day.

His law concerning the sabbath day says, "Remember the sabbath day, to keep it holy. Six days you shall labor and do all your work, but the seventh day is the sabbath of the LORD your God. *In it* you shall do no work: you, or your son, or your daughter, or your male servant, or your female servant, or your cattle, or your stranger that is within your gates. For in six days the LORD made the heavens and the earth, the sea, and all that is in them, and rested the seventh day. Therefore the LORD blessed the sabbath day, and hallowed it" (Exodus 20:8–11). So, for man, God again placed the emphasis of the seventh (sabbath) day on rest.

God also commanded His people to observe this periodic rest. He did so by commanding that all debts owed be cancelled on the seventh year. This is also carried forward to include setting free any slave on the seventh year (Exodus 21:2; Deuteronomy 15:1, 12).

God commanded the law of sabbath of rest which applies to God and man to also apply to the earth. Hence, He commanded that the land shall be cultivated continuously for six years. But on the seventh year, the land shall be left fallow for it to observe its sabbath of rest (Leviticus 25:4; 26:34–35). Failure of the Israelites to allow the land to rest continuously resulted in severe punishment. They were carried away into captivity in Babylon for seventy years (2 Chronicles 36:21; Jeremiah 25:11). Each year of their captivity represented seven years of disobedience of God's commandment. And during that lengthy period of seventy years, the land kept her sabbath. This shows that they had continuously disobeyed the law of the sabbath of rest for 70x7 years. This is equal to 490 years. God is indeed longsuffering!

Through the trinity and the sabbath of rest, God confirms the unity or oneness of the universe. The unity or oneness consists of the Creator and the created or the Maker and the made. There is no type of equilibrium or stability that can compare with that unity or oneness.

What a Living Soul Means

The adjective, "living," which qualifies the soul, is a present continuous tense. This tense means that the man, as a soul, cannot die from the moment God formed him. Ecclesiastes 3:14 confirms this undying attribute of man. It says, "I know that whatever God does, it shall be forever. Nothing can be added to it, and nothing taken from it. God does *it*, that men should fear before Him." Because God created man in His own image and likeness, each of the three sequential components of man, which are body, soul, and spirit, must have its equivalent part in God.

The Image and Likeness of God

That man became "a living soul" is the first image and likeness of God which he depicted. This is by His introduction severally as "the living God". For example, Simon Peter, by revelation of the Father, says that Jesus is the Christ, the Son of "the living God" (Matthew 16:16; John 6:69).

The high priest, Caiaphas, also addressed Him as such. This was during the trial of Jesus. Jesus did not respond to what some people witnessed against Him. The high priest then said to Him: "…I put You under oath by "the living God": that You tell us if You are the Christ, the Son of God" (Matthew 26:63).

Jesus also addressed the Father as "the living God". He told His disciples, "As 'the living Father' has sent Me, and I live by the Father: so he that eats Me, even he shall live by Me" (John 6:57). The phrase, "the soul of man", therefore, points to the Father as being "the Soul of God". Man is "a living soul", and the Father, who is otherwise called "the living God", is also "the Soul of God". Hence man has only one Father. Jesus asserts this relationship between man and God in Matthew 23:9. In the text, Jesus says, "Do not call anyone on earth your Father; for One is your Father, He who is in heaven."

There Is another Type of Seed

There is another type of seed. It is unlike the one which is described in Genesis 1:29a, which I had classified as invisible to the human eyes. This other type can be seen by man. It is described in Genesis 1:29b. The text says, "…and every tree whose fruit yields seed; to you it shall be for food." This other type of seed has two types. The first of the two types is visible. An example of it is cashew nut which has its seed externally attached to its succulent fruit. The second of the two types of seeds are located inside the succulent fruits. They are visible only when their outer coverings, skin and succulent parts, are ripped open. Examples of this second type are apple, cherry, and mango.

This second type of seed, which is visible, and has succulent fruit, typifies Jesus. Therefore, though Jesus possessed body, He is the visible God, just as the invisible seed typifies God. Therefore, Jesus, the visible God is the Body of God, who is the Word that was made flesh (John 1:14).

Hebrews 2:14 further confirms this very important connection with man. It says, "Inasmuch then as the children have partaken of flesh and blood, He Himself likewise shared in the same, that through death He might destroy him who had the power of death, that is, the devil."

According to Ezekiel 18:4, "... the soul that sins, it shall die." But because Jesus did not commit any sin that warranted that He should have died, hence, He was resurrected on the third day. And having died once and was resurrected, He shall not die anymore. He, thereby, conquered death.

The Spirit of Man Cannot Be Seen

The force or power that holds the visible soil and the invisible seed in the dust of the ground together, even though loosely, is also invisible. When God formed man, He introduced into him a type of that force or power. It came through His breath which He breathed into his nostrils. The breath became the spirit of man. It holds his visible body and unseen soul together. And because man is the image and likeness of God, therefore, "the Spirit of God" is, also, invisible. It also holds "the visible Body of God" and "the invisible Soul of God" together.

The Spirit of God is, thus, equally possessed by Jesus, who is the visible Body of God, and the Father, who is the invisible Soul of God. Hence, Apostle John, by the same Spirit of God could say in 1 John 4:2–3, "By this know you the Spirit of God: every spirit that confesses that Jesus Christ has come in the flesh is of God, and every spirit that does not confess that Jesus has come in the flesh is not of God. And this is the *spirit* of the Antichrist, which you have heard was coming, and is now already in the world."

The Soul of Man Is "The Only True Man"

When the body of a man dies, it returns to the dust from which it was taken. The spirit also returns to God who gave it through His breath, which He breathed into man's nostrils at his formation. So, of the two original components of man, body and soul, which came from the soil and seed respectively, it is the latter, that continues to live. This shows that the soul of man which is invisible is eternal in its existence. This is a witness to it becoming a living soul at its formation in Genesis 2:7.

Paul witnesses to the eternal nature of the soul in 2 Corinthians 4:17–18. The text says, "For our light affliction, which is but for a moment, is working for us a far more exceeding *and* eternal weight of glory, while we do not look at the things which are seen, but at the things which are not seen. For the things which are seen *are* temporal, but the things which are not seen *are* eternal." Therefore, the soul of man, which is invisible, and is thus eternal, is "the only true man." We can, therefore, infer from the fore going that "the Soul of God" is "the only true God." This truth is what Jesus affirms in John 17:3 by describing the Father as the only true God.

Jesus Confirms the Soul as "The Only True Man"

The Scripture says that by the mouth of two or three witnesses every word may be established (Matthew 18:16; 2 Corinthians 13:1). Therefore, the truth stated above shall be witnessed to by Jesus.

First, the Father had revealed to Peter that Jesus is the Christ, the Son of the living God, and he had so declared it. Jesus had also blessed him for the revelation he received. Thereafter, He began to inform the disciples that He must suffer and be killed in Jerusalem. The same Peter began to rebuke Him for agreeing to suffer and be killed. In the course of His reaction against Peter's rebuke, Jesus confirms that the soul is the only true man.

This truth can be gleaned from two identical questions of Jesus in Mark 8:36 and Luke 9:25. In the first text, He asks, "For what will it profit a man if he gains the whole world, and loses his own soul?" In the second text, He asks, "For what profit is it to a man if he gains the whole world, and is himself destroyed or lost?" By the two identical questions, Jesus equates "the soul of a man" with "himself". Therefore, the soul of man is the only true man.

Second, when His crucifixion was imminent, He went with His disciples into the Garden of Gethsemane to pray. He left Peter, James, and John somewhere in the Garden away from the other eight and ordered them to stay and watch with Him. When He came back after His first of three rounds of prayer, He met them sleeping. He addressed Peter, in particular, saying, "What? Could you not watch with Me one hour? Watch and pray, lest you enter into temptation. The spirit indeed *is* willing, but the flesh *is* weak" (Matthew 26:40–41).

Spirit and flesh (body) are two of the three components that make up a man. The spirit came from God through His breath of life. The body, as already repeatedly stated, came from the visible soil. The soul, which came from the invisible seed in the dust of the ground, is the third component of man that is not mentioned by Jesus. And, it is the component of man that both the spiritual and physical realms desire to influence. The spiritual realm tries to influence it through man's spirit. The physical realm, also, tries to influence it through his body. The soul of man is, thus, the only true man. And because man is the image and likeness of God, therefore, God is also the only true God.

Jesus Had To Be Resurrected from the Dead

The prophecy of King David in Psalm 16:10 says, "For You will not leave my soul in Sheol, nor will You allow Your Holy One to see corruption." This is another prophecy that Jesus came to fulfill. In order to establish the truth of Jesus being God, He had to be resurrected from the dead. From the moment that Jesus as "the Body of God" was resurrected, He overcame death. He also became incorruptible, and eternal. Therefore, as "the Body of God," Jesus thus became the visible part of the true God, who is "the Soul of God." And He went back to heaven to become one with the Father.

A derivative of this truth is that when the body of a man dies, it must also be resurrected for it to become one with his soul. If such a soul had been in hell, that is where the resurrected body will go and join with it to become one. In the alternative, if such a soul had been in heaven, that is also where his resurrected body will go and join with it to become one.

Proof of Who the Trinity of God Are

My next assignment is to show who the three Persons of the Trinity of God are. Meanwhile, they have been described as "The Body of God" (John 1:14; Colossians 2:8–9), "The Soul of God" (John 1:18; 5:37), and "The Spirit of God" (Genesis 1:2). These descriptions have been derived from the example of man who is the image of God (Genesis 1:26–27). The event of the baptism of Jesus with water by John will be used to show who they are.

Jesus came from Nazareth in Galilee to River Jordan unto John, to be baptized. John, initially, was not willing to baptize Him. Instead, he reckoned that Jesus was the one that should baptize him. But Jesus, in the record of Matthew, said to him, "Suffer it to be so now: for thus it becomes us to fulfill all righteousness." The first person plural pronoun, "us," in the quote above refers to the three Persons who were to be involved in this baptism apart from John.

John baptized Jesus with the water of River Jordan by immersing Him into it. Jesus went up straightway out of the water: and, lo, the heavens were opened unto Him. John, then, saw the Spirit of God, like a dove, descend and remain upon Him. This was how Jesus received the Spirit without measure (John 3:34). Suddenly a voice *came* from heaven, saying, "This is My beloved Son, in whom I am well pleased."

John the Baptist clearly identified Him to be Jesus by His body which he saw, and the brief discussion which they earlier had. He, thereafter, testified as recorded in John 1:33–34, "I did not know Him, but He who sent me to baptize with water said to me, 'Upon whom you see the Spirit descending, and remaining on Him, this is He who baptizes with the Holy Spirit.' And I have seen and testified that this is the Son of God."

The descent of the Spirit like a dove upon Jesus confirms the partnering of Him (the Spirit) with Jesus. The partnering was done by the Owner of the voice that John heard. You cannot give what you do not have. The Person that could partner the Spirit with someone else must be God, who Himself is a Spirit (John 4:24). And to the extent of addressing Jesus as, "My beloved Son, in whom I am well pleased," the Owner of the voice must be the Father of Jesus.

Jesus informed His disciples about two types of baptism before He ascended back to heaven. He said as recorded in Acts 1:5, "For John truly baptized with water, but you shall be baptized with the Holy Spirit not many days from now." For Jesus to baptize people with the Holy Spirit means to literally take them and dip them into the Holy Spirit as John dipped people in water. Therefore, for Jesus to baptize people by dipping them into the Holy Spirit/ Ghost, He must have a body like John. This is an additional proof that Jesus is, indeed, "the Body of God." And for Him to dip a person into the Holy Spirit/Ghost whom a man cannot see, He must be God.

Jesus earlier promised to pray the Father to give the disciples the Spirit of truth. He is otherwise called another Helper or Comforter. According to Jesus, there are two different positions that He can be in His association with the disciples. One is that He may abide with them forever. Meanwhile, He dwells with them. To abide or dwell with someone are identical in meaning. Two is that He will be in them (John 14:16–17). Two sets of truths are derivable from this association.

The first truth is that the Spirit of God or Spirit of truth will act like a Person who can abide or dwell with someone as a companion or partner. The Spirit of God or the Spirit of truth, like a dove, had played this role of a companion to Jesus. The second is that the Spirit of God or the Spirit of truth can also appear like wind, water, and fire. So, the Holy Spirit/Ghost shall be on the inside, while the Spirit of truth, shall be on the outside of a person.

The Holy Spirit and the Spirit of God Speak Differently

Jesus, towards the end of His earthly mission, stressed the need to preach the gospel to all the nations. Specifically, He says as recorded in Mark 13:11, "But when they arrest *you* and deliver you up, do not worry beforehand, or premeditate what you will speak. But whatever is given you in that hour, speak that; for it is not you who speak, but the Holy Spirit." A man speaks from the inside of him. Therefore, the Holy Spirit from the inside of men speaks out in unknown tongues (Acts 2:4). The Spirit of God or the Spirit of truth, on the other hand, from the outside speaks to people. His spoken word is called *Rhema*. Such communication is lifted from *logos*, the written word of God. I have a testimony in this regard.

I was once in a dilemma, on a particular day, as to which of two programs I should attend. The first was the burial ceremony of a relative of a member of my church members. The second was a seminar that was organized by a branch of Pentecostal Fellowship of Nigeria (PFN). I was advised by someone to attend the former event first. The person's reason for such advice was because it involved a member of my immediate constituency. But, surprisingly, I clearly heard the Spirit of God say to me, "Let the dead bury their dead."

Jesus once invited someone to follow Him. Instead of instantly obeying, he said, "Lord, let me first go and bury my father" (Luke 9:60). The statement that I heard "Let the dead bury their dead" was what Jesus said to that fellow. The Spirit of God lifted it. It became *Rhema* and said it to me. By this timely *Rhema* from Him, I deduced that God wanted me to attend the seminar first. I obeyed and was tremendously blessed by a particular message during the seminar. Surprisingly, I was also able to attend the former event.

In continuation of the narrative of the event at the baptism of Jesus, a voice from above said, "This is My beloved Son, in whom I am well pleased." Therefore, the voice must be that of a Father as well as the Father. Hence, He could call Jesus His beloved Son. John only heard the voice. It introduced Jesus, who has been proved to be God, as His beloved Son in whom He, the Father, is well pleased. It is thus proved that the Owner of the voice could not be less than God. And for calling Jesus, "My beloved Son," He must be the Father of Jesus.

Furthermore, because John did not see Him, the Speaker can be called "The Soul of God." This makes the Speaker, the Father of Jesus, to be like "the soul of man," which cannot be seen. From this analysis, it becomes clear that the name of the Person described as "The Soul of God" is "the Father."

Furthermore, the name of the Person described as the "The Spirit of God" or "the Spirit of truth" who appeared in the form of a dove is "the Spirit." The name of this third Person, however, must also be confirmed, and it is so confirmed by the event that followed.

The record of Matthew of the event says, "Then Jesus was led up by the Spirit into the wilderness to be tempted by the devil" (Matthew 4:1). In this text, the name of the Spirit of God is shortened to "the Spirit." The record of the same event by Luke is a bit more elaborate. It says, "Then Jesus, being filled with the Holy Spirit, returned from the Jordan and was led by the Spirit into the wilderness" (Luke 4:1). On that occasion, Jesus had the Spirit as a Companion who held His hand and led Him. In addition, He had the Holy Spirit inside of Him as air or wind for empowerment.

For the Spirit, who cannot be seen, to hold the hand of Jesus, who has been proved to be God, and who could be seen, must also be God.

He held Jesus' hand and led Him into the wilderness to be tested by the devil. The Spirit, therefore, acted like a Person.

Jesus started to fast as soon as He got into the wilderness. He continued the exercise for forty days. His fast, no doubt, attracted the attention of the devil. He, therefore, came to Him to test Him when He was hungry. The timing of the test was aimed at taking advantage of the weakness of His flesh. But Jesus passed the three satanic tests by quoting the Word of God. There are, therefore, three clearly identified Persons at the baptism of Jesus. They are, Jesus, the Father, and the Spirit, each of who is God. Yet, Jesus came forth from the Father and came into the world (John 16:28). They are, therefore, three distinct Persons that make up the "God of Abraham."

Jesus described God the Father as the only true God (John 17:3). Yet each of Jesus and the Spirit is also God. This description suggests that the phrase, "the only true God," has a deeper meaning. It suggests that Jesus, the Father, and the Spirit are one. This is why the "God of Abraham" is described as Trinity.

Of these three Persons, the first two, the Father and Jesus, are one (John 10:30). They are like the invisible seed and the visible soil in the dust of the ground, respectively, but which are one. They are also like the invisible soul and visible body of man which are one. This type of oneness is replicated by the Spirit and the Holy Spirit, who also are one. And because God the Father is a Spirit (John 4:24), therefore, Jesus, who is one with Him, is also a Spirit. It is no wonder that He is called Emmanuel, a name that means "God with us" (Matthew 1:23).

Each of the three, namely, Father, Jesus, and Spirit is, therefore, not only a Person, but also a Spirit. The three Spirits can be likened to oxygen, nitrogen, and carbon dioxide each of which is a gas and together also called air. As gasses in combination, each maintains its unique identity and characteristic. The Trinity of God is like that. In view of the proof of each of the Father, Jesus, and the Spirit being a

Spirit, therefore, the concept of "the Trinity of God" can also be called "the Trinity of Spirit".

Apostle Paul could, therefore, by the same Spirit declare in 1 Timothy 3:16, "And without controversy great is the mystery of godliness: God was manifested in the flesh, justified in the Spirit, seen by angels, preached among the Gentiles, believed on in the world, received up in glory." Believe this biblical record and be blessed.

Establishment of the Church

Jesus once told His disciples about the willingness of the Father to give them good gifts. He asked in Luke 11:13, "If you then, being evil, know how to give good gifts unto your children: how much more shall *your* heavenly Father give the Holy Spirit to them that ask Him?"

The three Persons or Spirits, namely, the Father, Jesus, the Spirit, played active roles in the establishment of the Church. They did in collaboration with the Holy Spirit or Holy Ghost that is like wind, living water, and tongues of fire. Hence, the Scripture says, and "When the Day of Pentecost had fully come, they were all with one accord in one place. And suddenly there came a sound from heaven, as of a rushing mighty wind, and it filled the whole house where they were sitting. Then there appeared to them divided tongues, as of fire, and *one* sat upon each of them. And they were all filled with the Holy Spirit and began to speak with other tongues, as the Spirit gave them utterance" (Acts 2:1–4).

The Father approved the whole operation and, instantly, they went about preaching the resurrection of Jesus with power. These three Persons, the Father, Jesus, and the Spirit, were involved with building the Church of Jesus. Therefore, any religion that lacks their involvement in its establishment, and empowered by the Holy Spirit, is an empty one.

Jesus is from everlasting. He had no beginning. He is Alpha and Omega (Revelation 1:8). And He shall have no end. From everlasting, He had been in the form of man. The reasons for being in the form of man are two-fold. The first is so that He might provide the sacrifice for the remission of sin which man was sure to commit. By His sacrifice, He shall then deliver man from satanic bondage (Hebrews 2:9–18). The second reason is that man might be created in His image.

This image consists of body, soul, and spirit that became the three parts of man. Jesus can then use that image as a teaching aid to help man understand the Bible and thereby make God known. The knowledge of God by man will then give him eternal life. But, somehow, multitudes and multitudes of peoples do not believe in the concept of trinity. Most of those who believe, do not even understand it. Worst of all, a multitude of peoples do not believe that Jesus is God. This is a tragedy of unimaginable dimension.

"Eating the Flesh of Jesus and Drinking His Blood"

Jesus came to the world and opened His mouth in parables (Matthew 13:35) so as to fulfill the prophecy of David in Psalm 78:2. The text in NKJV says, "I will open My mouth in a parable; I will utter dark sayings of old...." I shall give two examples of dark sayings, which imply sayings with hidden meaning.

First, in John 6:51, He informed the Jews and His disciples, "I am the living bread which came down from heaven. If anyone eats of this bread, he will live forever; and the bread that I shall give is My flesh, which I shall give for the life of the world." The Jews reacted negatively to these words. They wondered how He could give His flesh to them to eat. They did not recognize that He was speaking in parable.

He then said to them in John 6:53–56, "Most assuredly, I say to you, unless you eat the flesh of the Son of Man and drink His blood, you have no life in you. Whoever eats My flesh and drinks My blood has eternal life, and I will raise him up at the last day. For My flesh is food indeed, and My blood is drink indeed. He who eats My flesh and drinks My blood abides in Me, and I in him." This saying caused them to desert Him. The disciples also, almost did. Judas Iscariot, however, had already deserted Him in his heart.

In order to understand the parable of eating His flesh and drinking His blood, Jesus must be believed to be like the second type of seed in Genesis 1:29b. The succulent outer part of the fruit, when broken and eaten, provides continuous healthy bodily living for man on earth. The Father, who is God, is like the invisible seed in the dust of the ground. Jesus, the Son, who is like the visible seed, but which is hidden in the succulent outer part, must also be God. Both invisible and visible seed have identical components. The components include seed coat, embryo, and cotyledon (endosperm).[8]

This parable relates to the Holy Communion which Jesus inaugurated to bring about the New Covenant. His body which is "broken" at the Holy Communion table is like the succulent part of the fruit. The juice in this outer part is like His blood which is shed for the remission of the sin of mankind. And as man needs the succulent part of fruit to live a healthy life on earth, so does he need the flesh and blood of Jesus for eternal spiritual living in heaven. His being God, therefore, is strongly connected with His being crucified and resurrected.

The Body of God Is God, therefore, Jesus Is God

Second, He told His disciples in John 15:5, "...without Me you can do nothing." This is a parable in which the unparalleled role of Jesus in the affairs of God and man is hidden.

The trinity of man consists of body, soul, and spirit. These three parts constitute the image and likeness of God. The corresponding parts

[8] https://www.google .com

of God, as has been repeatedly emphasized in this chapter are, Body of God, Soul of God, and Spirit of God. The Body of God corresponds with the body of man. The body of man is the visible part of him. Therefore, the visible part of God, as has been proved, is Jesus, who can be seen. His position and identity among the Trinity of God thus correspond with the position and identity of the body of man among the trinity of man.

A man cannot do anything practically, such as writing and walking, without a part of his body. Similarly, God will not do anything practically, in His relationship with man, without Jesus, "the Body of God." The Body of God is God; therefore, Jesus is God.

God Desires We Believe that He Exists

Finally, God desires that we believe that He exists even though we do not see Him. This is the message of God in Hebrews 11:6. It says, "But without faith it is impossible to please Him (God): for he that comes to God must believe that He is, and that He is a rewarder of them that diligently seek Him." This scriptural requirement can be proved with the unseen seed.

If we insist on seeing the unseen seed before believing that they are in a particular soil, it can be shown, somehow. This is by setting apart a scoop of the soil. We can then wet it with water. In course of time, some plant will germinate out of that soil. The germinated plant is vivid evidence that, hitherto, there was seed in that soil, even though not seen.

Seeing a thing before believing that it exists is not faith but knowledge. God desires that we believe that He exists like the unseen seed even though we do not see Him. This is what sets the tone for our relationship with Him.

God, however, did the kind of thing that can be done with soil. He brought forth His Son, Jesus, into the world, by a supernatural conception. He was also crucified and was resurrected. Yet, most of mankind does not believe that God has a Son!

CHAPTER 10

Surprising Declarations of Jesus

Jesus and Religion Differentiated

This chapter is meant to further prove that Jesus is the only Savior of the world and not religion. Religion, however, has its good purpose for someone who has, first of all, been saved by the Lord Jesus Christ.

Psalm 37:3 says, "Trust in the LORD, and do good…." These are two commands of God. The first says, "Trust in the LORD." It is spiritual. It requires a person to believe that what God says is true. It is also a requirement for enjoyment of God's blessings.

But how can it be known that someone trusts or believes in the LORD? It can be known by the person acting in obedience to what God commands. If someone, therefore, does not trust in the LORD, he will not obey His command. This means that he will not be enabled to do what God expects him to do. This also means that such a person is disobedient. The result of his disobedience is that he will not enjoy the benefit of obedience of God's command.

One important benefit of obedience of God's command is salvation of one's soul. Psalm 37:39–40 confirms the reality of this benefit of obedience. It says, "But the salvation of the righteous *is* from the LORD; *He is* their strength in the time of trouble. And the LORD shall help them and deliver them; He shall deliver them from the wicked, and save them, because they trust in Him."

The promise of salvation for those who trust in Him is confirmed by God's command that a person must be born again so as to be saved (John 3:3, 5). And this salvation can be gotten only through Jesus whom someone must believe in so as not to perish (John 3:16). It then means that whoever chooses to be born again can be described as someone who trusts in the LORD.

The second command which says, "…and do good…" is physical. It commands the person who trusts in God to show it by doing good works. But it is when a man is born again that his works can be adjudged by God to be good. This is because he will not do the works by his might or power but by the Spirit of the LORD of hosts (Zechariah 4:6). Such good works come under what is called religion. Hence pure and undefiled religion is to do good works according to Apostle James (James 1:27). Several other good works are mentioned by Jesus Christ in Matthew 25:32–40.

Psalm 37:3, 39–40 thus clearly differentiates Jesus and religion. For, through the former, a man is saved, and through the latter, he is enabled to do good works by exercising genuine love. But should a man dare to neglect to be saved or born again, his "good work" cannot earn him salvation. This is because they will be done by his might and power. Such a "righteous work" is at best like filthy rag (Isaiah 64:6). This is because it will lack the input of the Spirit of God which can only be enjoyed by being first of all born again.

Apostle Peter, in 1 Peter 1:22–23, sheds light on the role of the Spirit of God and the Holy Ghost. According to the text, a person is born again through a process. The first step in the process is to obey the truth of the word of God. The second step is that the Spirit of God purifies the soul of such a person. The third is that love for the brethren is shed abroad in the heart of the person by Jesus baptizing him with the Holy Ghost. The fruit of the Spirit will start to manifest in him. A man as a living soul, who is not purified by the truth, goes to hell after his soul and body are separated as a result of the death of his body.

"Not Peace but Division"

Jesus made a surprising statement in Luke 12:51–53. It is entitled "Not Peace but Division" in the edition of a KJV Bible, published by the Bible Society of Nigeria. The text says: "Do you suppose that I came to give peace on earth? I tell you, not at all, but rather division. For from now on five in one house will be divided: three against two, and two against three. Father will be divided against son and son against father, mother against daughter and daughter against mother, mother-in-law against her daughter-in-law and the daughter-in-law against her mother-in-law." In order to shed some light on the difference between Jesus and religion, this surprising statement will be examined.

If we take this statement of Jesus in isolation, we shall miss the lesson it has to teach. It requires a careful analysis in order to unravel its contribution to the message of this book. The message is about the inability of religion to save a person from perishing through sin. It teaches that Jesus is the only way to God, and hence, the only Savior of the world.

A Brief Explanation of the Surprising Statement

Before Jesus came, it can be assumed that the five people in that family were all adherents of one religion, most probably, Judaism. The five members of the group in this example were made up of one father, one mother, one son, one daughter, and one daughter-in-law. That there was one daughter-in-law means that the son had married. Therefore, the one group which existed in that family came through two processes, marriage, and birth. The son and the daughter were born into the religion of their father, which he and his wife, hitherto, must have been practising. The daughter-in-law, as to be expected, would most likely have embraced the religion of the son who became her husband. This was also how the father and the mother had been. Jesus, therefore, bears witness to the truth of birth being a means to come to be attached to any religion.

If all the five members of this family continued to practise that religion, there might, in all probability, be no division in that family. It might be peace and cordiality all the way. But if Jesus had not come to the world, their religion cannot save them. It is Jesus that can. They will thus perish after death.

But God did not cause them to be born into their religion so as to perish. He thus gave Jesus. And when He came into the world, He calls on all the five people to embrace Him as the only One that can give them salvation. Hence, He urged everyone to come unto Him. He would then give them rest. This is because His yoke is easy and His burden is light (Matthew 11:28–30).

If all the five members in this family choose to do so, there will continue to be peace and no division in that house. And if they eventually die, they will enter God's Kingdom. But a mass movement of members of any family into a relationship with Jesus is not always the case. Anyone of the five who desires the promised rest of Jesus can decide to heed His call. One, two, or three of them could so decide. Those in this category would qualify, according to Jesus' promise, to be raised up after their death (John 5:25). Consequently, they would not end in perdition like Judas Iscariot did. This would be a better option than that all the five should perish!

However, by their decision, which is called *Born again*, or "Believe also in Jesus," such a decision is usually met with persecution by the other members of the family. The persecution could, invariably, disrupt the peaceful atmosphere that had hitherto existed in the family. The persecution might even result in the expulsion of those that decide for Jesus. This happens most often when the leader, the father, as in this example, is against such a decision.

If those being persecuted for their decision, be they two or three, are not offended in Jesus, they will ultimately make it to eternal rest which He promises. If all the members decline to convert, the final result would be that all of them will perish after death. Therefore, by the coming of Jesus to the world, whereby two or three of them perish not after death, is the better of two options.

In order to successfully unravel the surprising statement, I shall associate it with three other declarations of Jesus. The first of these is the story of the rich man and Lazarus (Luke 16:19–31). The second is the news of the sudden death of some people, according to the record in Luke 13:1–5. The third is the Parable of the Net which is recorded in Matthew 13:47–50.

The Story of the Rich Man and Lazarus

The greater state of "no peace but division" which the coming of Jesus brought about will happen after death. His story of the rich man and Lazarus in Luke 16:19–31 addresses this truth. Lazarus, who suffered untold hardship on earth, died. His soul was carried into Abraham's bosom. The rich man, who lived a prosperous life but totally neglected the poor Lazarus at his door step, also died, and was buried. Both the poor and rich died.

The reality was that the bodies of both Lazarus and the rich man were buried in the earth. But why is it reported that the rich man was buried in the earth and Lazarus was carried up into Abraham's bosom? It was because the rich man remained as flesh and blood that cannot inherit the kingdom of God (1 Corinthians 15:50). His soul was not converted to a new creature with old things passed away when he was on the earth. This was the mercy that Lazarus enjoyed.

It is in Jesus that anyone could become a new creation. It is in Him alone that the "old things" of man can pass away (2 Corinthians 5:17). They pass away when someone believes in Him or enjoys God's mercy. Hence, Jesus instructed His disciples as to who to fear in the course of preaching the Kingdom of God. He said, "And do not fear those who kill the body but cannot kill the soul. But rather fear Him who is able to destroy both soul and body in hell" (Matthew 10:28).

According to *Complete Dictionary for Home and School* by International Bible Society, the verb "torment" means to treat cruelly and cause great suffering. It also means to tease or annoy. In hell, the rich man, as soul, started to suffer unending untold torment. Lazarus, also a soul that had become a new creation as angels of God, was carried into Abraham's bosom, a place of comfort.

When the body is eventually resurrected, it will merge with the soul which had hitherto been in hell. The situation of anyone, as the rich man, will start to suffer more terrible unending untold torment in hell. The body of anyone like Lazarus will also eventually resurrect. It will also merge with the soul which had hitherto been in heaven, a place of comfort.

Meanwhile, the rich man, as soul, saw Lazarus, also as a soul, in his new joyous state as against his sorrowful state on earth. He then requested Abraham, whom he called "Father", to have mercy on him. The desired mercy which he desperately needed is for Lazarus to dip his finger in water and come over to cool his tongue with a drop of it. He acknowledged that he was being tormented in flame. What can a drop of water do to lighten the thirst of such a man in a flame?

Abraham did not deny his claim to being his son, but as to helping him in his new terrible state was impossible. He told him of an existing gulf, a sure division, between where he was, and where Lazarus was. He said that it was not possible to cross from one side of the gulf to the other.

Since crossing over was impossible, he then requested Abraham to send Lazarus to the members of his family. He had five brothers on earth. He requested Abraham to send Lazarus to them to warn them of the reality of hell and heaven. They could then avoid coming into hell, a place of unending torment in flame.

Abraham's answer was educative. He told him, first and foremost, that the option he requested was also not possible. Second, the way to prevent them from ending in hell where he, the rich man of yesterday, was in the flames that would not quench, was to believe Moses, the prophets and to also repent. Third, if they did not believe in the Scripture, even if anyone went back from heaven to warn them, they would not believe.

The sin of Adam brought sure death upon mankind. The division that Jesus brought is meant to enable whoever believes in Him to make it to heaven after death. Therefore, if Jesus had not come, everybody on earth would have ended in hell. Once this division into hell or heaven takes place after death, nothing can reverse it. There is no repentance after death. Hebrews 9:27 confirms this truth. It says, "And as it is appointed for men to die once, but after this the judgment, so Christ was offered once to bear the sins of many. To those who eagerly wait for Him, He will appear, a second time, apart from sin, for salvation." Once the judgment of a dead man takes him to hell, it cannot be appealed. It is a permanent judgment. The foregoing shows that Jesus is the Person that divides people, after they die, into either hell where there is torment in flames, or heaven where there is joy and rejoicing. He physically proved this by what He did to one of the two malefactors that were crucified with Him. He took the one that pleaded for mercy with Him to paradise and left the other to go and face the ordeal of hell fire.

News of Sudden Death of Some People

Adding one's belief in Jesus with one's belief in God is another definition of repentance. This essential spiritual need of man is well articulated by Jesus' response to a front-page news item in what I may call *Galilee*

Post. The news item in Luke 13:1–3 was about some Galileans whose blood the Roman governor Pilate mingled with their sacrifices.

These Galileans were, no doubt, very religious individuals. They had gone to Jerusalem to offer sacrifices. It could have been trespass, sin, peace, burnt, thanksgiving, or any offerings for that matter. They had gone to the temple with their animals for the purpose of cleansing. Governor Pilate decided to disrupt their religious ceremonies. As if doing so was not bad enough, he further ordered them killed. And to add insult to injury, he ordered that their blood be mingled with their sacrifices. It was a day of mixed bloods. The blood of men was mixed with that of some sacrificial animals.

If the event happened today, I imagine that the reporter of *Galilee Post* would have pointed the microphone at Jesus for Him to comment on the "sacrilege" cum murder which Pilate committed. Without the facility of a microphone, Jesus, however, answered, "Do you suppose that these Galileans were worse sinners than all *other* Galileans, because they suffered such things? I tell you, no; but unless you repent you will all likewise perish."

Jesus meant three things by His surprising response. The first thing is implied. It is that death will come when it will come. The second is that death is no respecter of persons. It comes to rich and poor, saint and sinner, at any time, anyhow, anywhere, and, uninvited. But what follows after death is what matters most. The third is what Jesus revealed about the end of these Galileans. He said that they perished.

Repentance, which will save everybody from perishing after death, is what should be carried out prior to dying. Jesus used the verb "perished", which is past tense, to mean that they ended their journeys in perdition. He meant that they went into hell like what happened to Judas Iscariot. What a sad way to end a religious practice despite the confidence they might have had in its power to *save* (italics for emphasis).

Jesus went further to show that He was up to date with the news in town. He thus further confirmed the need for repentance because death can happen to anybody, anytime, anywhere, and anyhow. He confirmed it by telling them another story in a few words. The story which is recorded in Luke 13:4–5 says, "Or those eighteen on whom the tower in Siloam fell and killed them, do you think that they were worse sinners than all *other* men who dwelt in Jerusalem? I tell you, no; but unless you repent you will all likewise perish."

Death is no respecter of persons. It comes to rich and poor, saint and sinner, at any time, anyhow, anywhere, and, uninvited.

Those eighteen persons were perhaps on vacation. They had gone to swim in the Olympic-sized swimming pool of their hotel. They had had one or two rounds of swimming. They were then sun-bathing preparatory to going for another warm round. Suddenly, the wall which surrounded the swimming pool collapsed and snuffed life out of them.

If this happened several years ago and mankind regards it as one of those fairy Bible tales, what shall we say of the terrible *tsunami* in Sumatra, Indonesia, of December 26, 2004, which suddenly left 227,898 dead?[9] Many of the victims were holiday makers from other countries. They had gone there on vacation but returned to their respective countries in body bags. Many of these tourists might have ended their journeys in heaven or hell depending upon their relationship with Jesus. Those who believed in Him ended their vacation in heaven. Those who knew Him not suddenly ended theirs in hell, their religions notwithstanding.

The Parable of the Net

The parable of the net by Jesus is a fitting conclusion to this narrative. Generally, the parables of Jesus focus on the Kingdom of Heaven or God. In the parable of the net in Matthew 13:47–50, He says, "Again,

[9] https://www.google.com [2004 Indian Ocean earthquake and tsunami]

the Kingdom of Heaven is like a dragnet that was cast into the sea and gathered some of every kind, which, when it was full, they drew to shore; and they sat down and gathered the good into vessels, but threw the bad away. So it will be at the end of the age. The angels will come forth, separate the wicked from among the just, and cast them into the furnace of fire. There will be wailing and gnashing of teeth."

Don't Be Firewood in Hell

The reality of this parable is that the sea into which the net shall be cast at the end of the world will be human beings. They shall be gathered by angels and divided into two groups. The first group will consist of those who believe in God only. It might surprise the reader that they would be termed the wicked despite their belief in God. The more surprising aspect is that they will be cast into the furnace of fire. And like the rich man above, they will be tormented in the furnace of fire. They will literally become the firewood which will be burning in hell forever. It is now that one is alive on earth that one can run away from being firewood in hell. The way out is by repenting so as to join the second group.

The second group will consist of those who believe in God and believe also in Jesus. They, too, will be gathered by the angels into vessels. The vessels are the mansions which Jesus had masterfully prepared to house them. So, while those in the former group are wailing and gnashing their teeth, the latter will be rejoicing, and dining and wining in the Kingdom of God. It is also here on earth that one can join this latter group.

Jesus, the Stone the Builder Rejected

Another very important surprising declaration of Jesus is that He is as the stone that the builder rejected which became the head of the corner (Matthew 21:42; Mark 12:10; Luke 20:17). This information calls to mind the rejection of Joseph, the eleventh son of Jacob, by his elder siblings. In order to prevent the actualization of his vision of leadership over them and the entire family, they sold him into slavery. But the vision which he narrated to them came to pass for the benefit of the entire family in Egypt several years later. In the same way, the rejection of Jesus warranted His condemnation and eventual crucifixion. But, it, ultimately, resulted in providing the precious blood for atonement for our souls (Leviticus 17:11).

Jesus is a unique Person. He told Nicodemus, "No one has ascended to heaven but He who came down from heaven, *that is,* the Son of Man who is in heaven" (John 3:13). Jesus was in heaven as the Son of God, the Word of God (John 1:1), but came down to earth by birth as the Son of Man (John 1:14). He, therefore, qualified to teach what He knew about heaven. He also qualified by His knowledge and understanding of the Law of Moses which spoke variously about Him. This is in particular with how Moses prophesied about the mode of death He would experience. Hence, He told Nicodemus, "And as Moses lifted up the serpent in the wilderness, even so must the Son of Man be lifted up, that whoever believes in Him should not perish, but have eternal life. For God so loved the world that He gave His only begotten Son, that whoever believes in Him should not perish but have everlasting life" (John 3:14–16). This Scripture implies that whoever believes *not* in Him would perish.

It is now that one is alive on earth that one can run away from being firewood in hell. The way out is by repenting....

Wow! This is a very hard saying. Why should they perish just for not believing in the Son of God, despite being born by God's approval? I suppose that this is a strong indication that Judaism, the religion of the Jews, cannot save anybody. And this is because…all have sinned and fallen short of the glory of God despite being born into belief in

God. This is also because at the level of "belief in God," no sacrifice has been made for them. *It is at the level of "belief also in Jesus" that the sacrifice for sin has been made and accepted* (italics for emphasis).

Jesus was like the Brazen Serpent

God fed the Israelites with manna in the wilderness in the course of their journey from Egypt to Canaan. They eventually murmured against God and Moses as they alleged that their soul is dried away by eating the manna (Numbers 11:6). They also murmured against them because of the way they went through in the wilderness (Numbers 21:4–9). On account of the second round of murmuring, God responded by sending serpents into their midst. Many of the people died as a result of snake bites!

They requested Moses to intercede for them. He did and God decided to stop their continual death on one condition. He instructed Moses to make a symbol of a snake with brass (bronze) and hang it on a pole. The brazen serpent represents the snake that bit the people because of their murmuring. It was, however, whoever looked at it that lived. Those that were bitten but did not look at the specially fabricated serpent died.

The picture of a snake on a pole is used to identify a hospital, a place of life and death. The venom of snake is known to possess both curative and deadly components. That Jesus had to connect His death to that Old Testament event is thus both stimulating and scary. It is stimulating because in it is life. It is scary because in it also is death. It is life for those that believe in the sacrifice of the precious blood of Jesus. It is death to those that do not believe in the same sacrifice. Eternal life and death are thus the embodiments of the cross of Jesus.

Jesus was not yet done with His surprising declaration. He said, "For God did not send His Son into the world to condemn the world, but that the world through Him might be saved. He who believes in

Him is not condemned; but he who does not believe is condemned already, because he has not believed in the name of the only begotten Son of God. And this is the condemnation, that light has come into the world, and men loved darkness rather than light, because their deeds were evil." This represented a major mission statement.

I think that Nicodemus benefited from this mission statement. It left an indelible mark on him. He became a secret disciple of Jesus. He and Joseph of Arimathaea played significant roles in the great task of giving the Lord Jesus a befitting burial after His crucifixion and death (John 19:38–42). If Nicodemus is in heaven, it will not be because he was a Pharisee, a leader of the Jews and an adherent of Judaism. Instead, it will be because he eventually believed in Jesus as the Son of God who was given for the salvation of mankind.

In addition, I believe that Nicodemus would have been rewarded by God for the good work he and Joseph of Arimathaea did for Jesus concerning His burial. It was like the good work a woman did when she poured alabaster box of ointment of spikenard on His head before His death. Jesus acknowledged that she would be rewarded by being spoken of for a memorial of her wherever the gospel will be preached (Mark 14:6–9). Such good works are integral part of religion, such as Judaism, which heaven will acknowledge, but not primarily for salvation.

Cornelius was very good at such religious acts. But they qualify only for a memorial and not for salvation. Cornelius thus needed help. Hence, Jesus sent Peter to him. He preached Jesus to him and his household. They believed, and He baptized them with the Holy Spirit as earlier stated (Acts 10:1–48).

We are not Robots on Earth

What everyone could not influence when coming to the world is the choice of which parents give birth to him or her. It also includes the religion, which I call "Belief in God," into which he or she is born. Having been in the world of good and evil, before dying, everyone is given a part to play. The part to play is to choose which side of eternity he or she returns to. Like what obtains on earth, there are also two parts in the hereafter. They are the good side and the evil. The good side is called heaven. The evil is hell. We are given a role to play because we are not robots on earth.

And having been in the world of good and evil for some time, we have basic knowledge of what is good and what is evil. We are then knowledgeable enough to choose between the two states. It is what we choose that we shall have.

God, however, decided to help us to make a good choice and not the evil. Hence, He says, "See, I have set before you today life and good, death and evil" (Deuteronomy 30:15). God showed that He is serious about His action. Hence, He further says, "I call heaven and earth as witness today against you, *that* I have set before you life and death, blessing and cursing; therefore choose life, that both you and your descendants may live" (Deuteronomy 30:19).

It is true that God made this commitment to Israel through Abraham, Isaac, and Jacob. In any case, He promised to bless the whole world through them (Genesis 12:1–3). So His promise applies to the entire human community.

Like what obtains on earth, there are also two parts in the hereafter. They are the good side and the evil. The good side is called heaven.

Families of Goodness and Evil

Everybody must make this critical choice before dying. God also pinpoints only two families either of which anyone can choose. One of these families is very rich in goodness while the other is very rich in evil. Jesus identified the two families in

John 10:10. They are the family of the "chief thief" and that of the "I AM," the Chief Shepherd. The "chief thief" comes not, except to steal, and to kill, and to destroy. The Chief Shepherd comes to give life on earth, and to give it abundantly in heaven. Everybody should be able to differentiate good deeds from evil ones. Whatever you don't want anyone to do to you is most likely to be evil. You, too, should not do the same to someone else. Do you want others to love you? Love others, too! It is what you sow that you shall reap ultimately. Sow good, and you shall reap more good than you sowed. It is the same with sowing evil. You reap more evil than you sow. Therefore, be very careful what type of seed you sow.

You have the choice to be born again on earth and end up in God's Kingdom of Light. You also have the choice to remain hooked on the lone religion into which you were born. Those who choose to remain hooked to that religion without believing in Jesus shall invariably end up in Satan's kingdom of darkness. If the latter is your destination, it will not be the fault of God, but yours.

You have the choice to be born again on earth and end up in God's Kingdom of Light. You also have the choice to remain hooked on the lone religion into which you were born.

Somewhere, someone asked Jesus an important question, to wit, "Lord, are there few who are saved?" Jesus answered the question, saying in Luke 13:24–28:

"Strive to enter through the narrow gate, for many, I say to you, will seek to enter and will not be able.

"When once the Master of the house has risen up and shut the door, and you begin to stand outside and knock at the door, saying, 'Lord, Lord, open for us,' and He will answer and say to you, 'I do not know you, where you are from,'

"Then you will begin to say, 'We ate and drank in Your presence, and You taught in our streets.'

> "But He will say, 'I tell you I do not know you, where you are from. Depart from Me, all you workers of iniquity.'
> "There will be weeping and gnashing of teeth, when you see Abraham and Isaac and Jacob and all the prophets in the kingdom of God, and you yourselves thrust out."

The reality of the statements above means that whichever religion one is born into, one must take the necessary step to be born again. It is, indeed, not religion that delivers people but Jesus.

Religious Activities without Jesus Are like Filthy Rags

James, one of the apostles of Jesus Christ, was inspired to say in James 1:26–27, "If anyone among you thinks he is religious, and does not bridle his tongue but deceives his own heart, this one's religion is useless. Pure and undefiled religion before God and the Father is this: to visit orphans and widows in their trouble, *and* to keep oneself unspotted from the world."

The statement above which is credited to James is not originally from him. He simply echoed the more elaborate version by Jesus in Matthew 25:34–46. But before Jesus made the fairly lengthy statement, He started, in His usual manner, with a parable. In the edition of the copy of my Bible, it is titled as the *Parable of the Talents*. But I choose to title it *The Parable of the Unprofitable Servant.*

A man was going to a far country and gave various talents to his three servants. He gave the first one five; the second two, and the third, one – everyone as per his ability. When he returned from his trip, he summoned the three servants to give account. The first one with five talents had gained five making a total of ten. The second one had gained two making a total of four. He commended both of them the same way and promised to make them rulers over many things.

The third servant with one talent did not make use of his. He described his master as a hard man who reaps where he has not sown.

He also gathers where he has not strawed. This servant was afraid of taking risk in business; therefore he hid the single talent in the earth. He only returned it to the man.

The master described him as wicked and slothful. He wondered why he did not give out his talent as loan so that he might get gain at his coming. The single talent was taken from him and given to the one with ten. He went down from owning one talent to zero, and was also called an unprofitable servant. Worst of all, he was cast into outer darkness where there shall be weeping and gnashing of teeth.

Jesus did not interpret this parable, but I presume that He is the Man. And the far country that He went to is heaven. This interpretation is confirmed by what followed the narrative of the parable. He shall return in His glory and all the holy angels with Him. He shall then sit upon the throne of His glory.

After all the nations would have been gathered together before Him, He shall separate them from one another. There shall be two groups, sheep and goats. He shall set the sheep on His right hand, but the goats on the left. He shall then address the two groups each at a time, from His royal throne, first, the sheep, which I would call "profitable servants," saying:

> "Come, you blessed of My Father, inherit the kingdom prepared for you from the foundation of the world:
> "For I was hungry, and you gave Me food; I was thirsty, and you gave Me drink; I was a stranger, and you took Me in;
> "I was naked and you clothed Me; I was sick, and you visited Me; I was in prison, and you came to Me."

The response of the first group, whom He called the "righteous," will be that of surprise as they will say,

> "Lord, when did we see You hungry and feed *You*, or thirsty, and give *You* drink?

"When did we see You a stranger, and take *You* in, or naked and clothe *You*?
"Or when did we see You sick, or in prison, and come to You?"
The answer of the King shall even be more surprising, as he will say to them,
"Assuredly, I say to you, 'Inasmuch as you did *it* to one of the least of these My brethren, you did *it* to Me.'"

The King shall then turn round to the second group on His left, the group of goats, which I would call "unprofitable servants," saying:
"Depart from Me, you "cursed," into the everlasting fire prepared for the devil and his angels:

"For I was hungry, and you gave Me no food; I was thirsty, and you gave Me no drink;
"I was a stranger, and you did not take Me in, naked, and you did not clothe Me, sick and in prison and you did not visit Me."
The members of this group shall equally respond, saying:
"Lord, when did we see you hungry or thirsty or a stranger or naked or sick or in prison, and did not minister to You?"
The answer of King Jesus shall be:
"Assuredly, I say to you, inasmuch as you did not do *it* to one of the least of these, you did not do *it* to Me."
The final judgment shall be:
"And these will go away into everlasting punishment, but the righteous into eternal life."

What Apostle James added to the activities that he and the Lord Jesus listed, which is of tremendous interest to me, is that he gives them a name. It is a name that is not once mentioned in the Old Testament. Apostle James calls them "religion," and those that practise them he describes as "religious."

As good as these activities are, without the input of Jesus, they are vain, useless or unprofitable. This is because nobody can keep himself unspotted from the world without the sacrifice which Jesus offered for the redemption of mankind. Therefore, religious activities without Jesus are like filthy rags. So, it is not by the religion into which a person is born that he can enter into heaven. It is true, indeed, that God without Jesus is the making of empty religion. It is like a broken cistern that can hold no water, in the words of Prophet Jeremiah (Jeremiah 2:13).

Please, do not stumble on this Jesus, the Rock of offence. Let Him be the Rock of ascent for you to mount up into the mansion that He has gladly gone ahead to prepare for you in His Father's house. Though He is the stone the builder rejected, that should not include you, dear reader.

CHAPTER 11

The Second Coming of Jesus

The Signs of the Coming of Jesus

There is a lack of understanding of the words of Jesus Christ with regard to His second coming. Two passages in the Scripture about it that theologians continue to debate are Matthew 24:36 and Mark 13:32.

Jesus and His disciples came out of the temple in Jerusalem. They had been touring the ancient religious edifice. Tourists to a building of such historic importance do not fail to reminisce on what they saw. They would discuss the iconic architectural wonders of such a building after returning to their hotel. So the disciples did.

They called His attention to the majestic standard of the second temple which Herod the Great had renovated and expanded. The disciples were, however, no doubt shocked when He said unto them, "Do you not see all these things? Assuredly, I say to you, not *one* stone shall be left here upon another, that shall not be thrown down." The disciples were no doubt terrified by the fate that awaited the magnificent temple.

Jesus later sat down upon the Mount of Olives and the disciples came to Him privately. For the disciples to have come to Him suggests that He seemed to be alone all by Himself. They came specifically to ask Him two questions. The first was: "Tell us, when will these things be?" They wanted to know when the destruction of the second temple will take place. [History has it that the temple was destroyed by the Roman army under Titus in AD 70.[10] He did not only destroy the second temple, but also much of the city of Jerusalem. This was about 40 years after Jesus' death and resurrection.]

[10] https://www.google.com

The second question did not have reference to the temple but to Him in person and the end of the world. They asked, "And what *will be* the sign of Your coming, and of the end of the age?" Let us clearly delineate the two signs. First, what *will* be the sign of His coming? Second, what *will* be the sign of the end of the age?

In answering their questions, Jesus listed several calamities that shall occur which will make up the signs of His coming. The signs will comprise a great number of fake Christs, of wars and rumors of wars and of nations rising up against nations. There will be famines and pestilences and earthquakes in diverse places. Believers in Christ will be delivered to be killed. Nations will rise up against the followers of Jesus. Many will betray one another and hate one another. False prophets will rise and deceive many. Iniquity will abound. As a result, the love of many will wax cold.

The signs are only showing that the end of the world is at hand. But it is after the gospel of the kingdom shall have been preached in the entire world for a witness unto all nations that the end will come (Matthew 24:14). This will be a milestone sign with reference to the coming of the Lord and the end of the world to watch out for. However, the auxiliary verb, "will", which qualifies the verb "come" in that text, strongly suggests that the end is not immediate. This is even after the gospel of the kingdom would have been preached in the entire world.

Jesus confirms this saying thus: "For then there will be great tribulation, such as has not been since the beginning of the world until this time, no, nor ever shall be" (Matthew 24:21).

Several other significant signs shall include the sign of the abomination of the desolation with reference to the vision of Daniel. His coming will not be in secret. For as lightning flashes from the east to the west and it is seen globally in the sky, so will his coming be. As carcases draw the attention of eagles to themselves (Matthew 24:28), so will His coming do. His coming will draw the attention of human souls to Him.

There will also be the sign of the darkening of the sun. This will result in perpetual darkness all over the globe. This phenomenon requires some explanation. The earth is spherical. If the time on one half of the globe is 12:00 noon, that particular side that faces the sun would have light while the other side would be in darkness. If the sun becomes darkened when that part of the earth is supposed to be facing the sun, then the sun would appear not to function. The result would be that there will be darkness globally. This will not be like an eclipse of the sun which darkens the earth partially and temporarily. The consequence will also be that there will be no moonlight since its main source of light, which it reflects, is the sun. The stars will also drop from the sky.

The sign of the Son of Man will appear in the heaven. I suppose that the sign of the Son of Man is the cross. Like He carried His cross, so He calls on whoever will come after Him to take up his cross, and follow Him (Matthew 16:24; Mark 10:21; Luke 9:23). This personalized sign will be followed with the coming of the Lord in the clouds of heaven. Jesus carried His cross on which He was later crucified, at least, part of the way to Golgotha. But this time around, His cross will not be for a second death. It will be meant to identify Him as the One that lay down His life for the sin of the world.

With the absence of the sun, moon, and stars, the Son of Man will then be the only source of light in the sky. Imagine seeing the form of a man in the sky, with the two arms stretched full length sideways, providing light in a very dark environment. By then the Son of God would be seen vividly as the light of the world which He had all along claimed to be (John 8:12; 9:5; 12:46). Then there will be the appearance of angels with trumpets to gather the elect (Matthew 24:31). Yet, all these signs would only show that the time of the end of the age is near even at the door (Matthew 24:33).

The prediction of the destruction of the temple came to pass. This is a positive indication that the prediction of the end of the age, and the coming of the Lord Jesus, will also come to pass. It does not matter whether the world likes it or not. It does not also matter whether the world believes the prediction of His Second Coming or not.

The Word, "Elect", Is Notable

The word, "Elect," is a notable word in the predictions concerning the Second Coming of Jesus. The word appears thrice in Matthew's record. The first time is in Matthew 24:22. It says, "And unless those days were shortened, no flesh would be saved; but for the elect's sake those days will be shortened." According to *Merriam Webster Dictionary*, as noun, because it refers to many people, *"elect's"*, is plural and not necessarily singular.

The second time is in Matthew 24:24. It says, "For false christs and false prophets will rise and show great signs and wonders to deceive, if possible, even the elect." Going by the explanation above, the phrase, "the elect", is also to be regarded as plural. The third time is in Matthew 24:31. It says, "And He will send His angels with a great sound of a trumpet, and they will gather together His elect from the four winds, from one end of heaven to the other." Gathering "His elect from the four winds..." confirms that the noun "elect" is, indeed, plural. Multitudes and multitudes of them shall be gathered from all over the world.

Ordinarily, the word "elect" as a verb is defined simply as "choose by vote." In a democracy, for example, people are elected to office by the majority of votes cast. When used as a noun, it stands for the person so chosen. In the spiritual realm, which is the context of this book, it means someone that is chosen. The choice is usually made by God. Two types of this word are mentioned in this book.

I. The Elect of God by Conception

The first type of elect is the conception of everybody that comes into the world. I describe it as the elect of God by conception. The first man and woman, Adam and Eve, were the only human beings created as adults. Every other person comes into the world through the process of a man and a woman mating.

It has been scientifically proven that the seeds which the man releases during copulation are in millions. The seeds are called semen (sperm plus seminal fluid from the prostate gland). The woman, on the other hand, releases, most often, only one ovum (egg) per month. It is only one of the seeds out of the lot that fertilizes the ovum. The rest naturally die.

The lone seed that succeeds out of the whole lot to fertilize the egg can be called, "the elect of God." That seed and the egg combine to form a fetus. It is then born at maturity as a human being, either male or female, into the family and religion of the parents. Such an elect of God is born into "belief in God."

II. The Elect of Jesus by Conversion

The second type of elect is the one by conversion of everybody that comes to Jesus. Such a person comes to Jesus by believing in Him to be the Son of God. This is in line with John 3:16 which says, "For God so loved the world that He gave His only begotten Son, that whoever believes in Him should not perish but have everlasting life." Such a person who decides to believe in Jesus as the Son of God is said to be born again. He is an elect of Jesus by conversion.

It is Jesus, according to Matthew 24:31, who shall send His angels with a great sound of a trumpet. They will gather together His elect from the four winds. You might ask, "What will be the lot of the numerous first set of elect of God by conception? Will they also be gathered?" If you have been following this narrative, your guess is as good as mine.

Because they came short of the glory of God and depended on religion to provide the shortfall, they would not qualify. If they are gathered at all, they will be deposited in hell. It is when one is still alive on the earth that one can take the vital step to be born again. After physical death, it shall no more be possible.

This Generation shall not Pass

At this point, Jesus struck a very clear tone, saying, "Assuredly, I say to you, this generation will by no means pass away till all these things take place" (Matthew 24:34). Which or what generation was He referring to?

Generations in history have several types of people. In the days of Jesus, one of the generations that existed and which had a lot of influence on the society was the Pharisee. A major characteristic of the Pharisees was the seeking for signs. Jesus once sighed deeply in His Spirit and asked, "Why does this generation seek a sign?" He then said, "Assuredly, I say to you, no sign shall be given to this generation" (Mark 8:12).

God had already given the signs of Noah and Jonah. Noah built an ark. He spent a long time inviting the people of his day into it so as to avoid perishing in the impending flood. They rejected his invitation and eventually perished in the flood that came (Genesis 6–9). God also sent Jonah to Nineveh with the message of repentance, otherwise they would be destroyed. Jonah chose to go to Tarshish. God sent a storm to trouble the ship. The cause of the storm was traced to Jonah. He told the mariners to throw him into the sea in order to stop the raging storm. No sooner they did than the storm ceased and a whale swallowed him. Jonah spent three days in the belly of the whale and was eventually vomited on the shore of Nineveh. The three days he spent in the whale was like the days that Jesus would spend in the earth before being resurrected. He was eventually crucified and buried. On the third day, God resurrected Him.

What further sign does the world want to have before believing that Jesus is the Son of God? God gave Him to the world in fulfillment of His promise (Genesis 3:15) and a series of prophecies. A few of such prophecies are documented in Genesis 22:7–8; Isaiah 7:14; 9:6–7; 53:2–12; and Micah 5:2. He was eventually made flesh through a very unique conception.

A vital question to ask is this: "Has that characteristic human trait of seeking signs changed now?" No. Jesus, however, does not want us to focus on signs but on His word which will not become void (Matthew 24:35).

Another characteristic of the generation of the days of Jesus which has persisted until now is being adulterous and sinful. Jesus declared, "For whoever is ashamed of Me and My words in this adulterous and sinful generation, of him the Son of Man also will be ashamed when He comes in the glory of His Father with the holy angels" (Mark 8:38).

Have men and women's adulterous and sinful ways changed? No. These ways have even attained more incredible dimensions beyond what God destroyed Sodom and Gomorrah for. The innate characteristics of generations of men and women have thus remained. And this is mainly because they are against being *"born-again."* They remained hooked on religion which could not save. And by the way, some people get hooked on their good works. They expect their good works to be able to save them. The Scripture describes such class of good works as filthy rags (Isaiah 64:6).

And yet another characteristic of that generation of the days of Jesus is faithlessness. Jesus identified this trait in the generality of the people and particularly His disciples. This was when He had just come down from the Mount of Transfiguration. He met a particular father in the midst of a crowd.

The father reported to Him how he had brought his son who was a lunatic to the disciples for deliverance but they could not help. Jesus then answered him and said, "O faithless generation, how long shall I be with you? How long shall I bear with you? Bring him to Me" (Mark 9:19). The father brought him to Jesus. He asked him for the history of the attack. His answer was that it had been from his childhood. The illness had tried severally to destroy him. He then said, "But if You can do anything, have compassion on us, and help us." This father pleaded a very important attribute of Jesus, which is compassion.

Jesus replied him thus: "If you can believe, all things *are* possible to him who believes." Jesus' statement shows that the issue of faithlessness also involves the people and not only the disciples. He delivered the boy. The disciples later sought to know why they could not handle the challenge. He informed them that such a challenge needed prayer and fasting to handle it.

Faithlessness has taken a worse turn today. Ministers and members of churches increasingly pretend to be godly these days. And this is basically because of what they would benefit from their services. They care less about the Second Coming of the Lord.

These are not all yet. Jesus identified another generation through His comment that followed the unexpected question that John the Baptist sent two of his disciples to ask Him. He had sent them from prison to ask Jesus if He was the one being expected or not. This unexpected question would have offended Jesus. If it was a trap of offense that Satan set for Jesus, He did not fall into it. He sent the two disciples back to report to John in prison what they saw happening. The blind are having their sight restored to them. Lepers are being cleansed, etc.

Jesus was no doubt disappointed by the message of John. So, after they left, He concluded with a fairly long speech about John the Baptist in Luke 7:24–28. He said, "What did you go out into the wilderness to see? *Is it* a reed shaken by the wind? But what did you go out for to see? *Is it* a man clothed in soft garment? Indeed those who are gorgeously apparelled and live in luxury are in kings' courts. But what did you go out to see? *Is it* a prophet? Yes, I say to you, and more than a prophet. This is *he*, of whom it is written: 'Behold I send My messenger before Your face, who will prepare Your way before You.' For I say to you, among those born of women there is not a greater prophet than John the Baptist; but he who is least in the Kingdom of God is greater than he."

Jesus said, among those born of women, there is not a greater prophet than John the Baptist. And if the least in the Kingdom of God is greater than him, can we then imagine how much greater than him Jesus is? This great prophet, John the Baptist, came and neither ate bread nor drank wine, and yet the people of his generation said that he had a devil. Jesus who is much greater than John the Baptist (Mark 1:7; Luke 3:16; John 1:27) came, ate, and drank, and the people of that generation called Him a gluttonous man, a winebibber, a friend of publicans and sinners (Matthew 11:19; Luke 7:34). Is that insulting characteristic any better nowadays? No. This ugly trait has assumed an uglier dimension. The internet with social media facilities has further heightened the tendency to insult people.

Apostle Paul carefully analyzes in 2 Timothy 3:1–5 the *Godlessness in the Last Days.* This characteristic is pointing to the imminent Second Coming of the Lord and the end of the age. We are called upon to watch so as not to be caught unawares. Going *paripassu* with the great tribulations shall be eating and drinking, marrying and giving in marriage. The end of the age shall then suddenly come as it did in the time of Noah. This was when the world was destroyed with flood as recorded in Genesis Chapters 7 and 8.

However, as to the exact day and hour of His second coming, and the end of the age, no one knows, not even the angels of heaven, but the Father only" (Matthew 24:36). Saint Mark also records the uncertain day and hour of these two future events in Mark 13:32. His record says, "But of that day and hour no one knows, not even the angels in heaven, nor the Son, but only the Father." The difference between the two records is the inclusion of the "Son" by Mark in his list.

Some commentators on these texts use the inclusion of the Son in the list to defend their doubt about the divinity of Jesus. Such people ask, "How can Jesus be God if He didn't know the day and the last hour that He Himself would come?" Someone explained that in His humanity, He would not know, but that in His divinity, He would know. But that Jesus does not know that day shows how much He made Himself of no reputation by coming to the world as a servant and like a man (Philippians 2:7).

Someone on *YouTube* tried to employ the tradition of the Jews to explain this poser. He noted that Jesus made that statement in the context of His coming marriage supper to which the saints shall be invited. He suggested that according to Jewish tradition, it was the father of the bridegroom that usually knew when the wedding of his son would take place, and not the son.

Jesus Spoke as the Person Sent

All those explanations fall far short of the truth of the statement of Jesus. For, when Jesus was on earth, He always spoke in the consciousness of the reality of the Trinity and eternity of God. He also always spoke very often in the consciousness of His position in the group as the Godhead bodily (Colossians 2:8–9). And most importantly, He [Jesus] also repeatedly spoke from the premise of the person that was *sent* [italics for emphasis]. In the gospel of John alone, He referred to Himself as being sent not less than thirty-four times. If added to the few passages in which Jesus says that He is sent in the other three synoptic gospels, they are not less than forty times that He acknowledged that He was sent. The reader can check these up in the following texts: Matthew 10:40; 15:24; Mark 9:37; Luke 4:18, 43; 10:16; John 4:34; 5:23, 24, 30, 36, 37, 38; 6:29, 38, 40, 57; 7:16, 28, 29, 33; 8:16, 18, 26, 29, 42; 9:4; 10:36; 11:42; 12:44, 45; 13:20; 14:24; 16:5; 17:3, 18, 21, 23, 25; and 20:21.

It is again as someone that would be sent that Jesus will come the second time. And it is not natural for someone to know when his or her sender would call on him or her to be sent. The only thing that he or she could know with certainty is that he or she would be sent. Even the angels knew this. This was why two of such messengers announced that Jesus would come again when He ascended back to heaven. But as to when exactly He would be sent, it is the sender that would have that information. However, this is not a strong defense for the Son not knowing the day of His coming. The strong defense is in the context of His role among the Membership of the Trinity of God.

The body of a man among the membership of the trinity of man does not know something until his soul has communicated it to it. This statement means that before the physical eyes of a man sees an object, the eyes of his soul would have first of all seen it. The eyes of his soul will then transmit what they see to his physical eyes. It is then that his physical eyes will see the object. The time that elapses between when the eyes of the soul see the object and when his physical eyes see it may be just a very split moment of time. Therefore, with Jesus being like the body of man, He cannot know something until the Father, who is like the soul of man, has communicated the knowledge to Him through the Spirit of God.

Jesus confirms this order of communication between Him and the Father during one controversy which He had with the Jews. He said, “I have many things to say and to judge concerning you, but He who sent Me is true; and I speak to the world those things which I heard from Him" (John 8:26). Earlier in His interaction with the Jews in Jerusalem, He had spoken along this format as recorded in John 5:30. He said, "I can of Myself do nothing. As I hear, I judge; and My judgment is righteous, because I do not seek My own will but the will of the Father who sent Me." He speaks what He hears from the Father. This is as the body of man, which is partly made up of the ear, hears what his soul says, and speaks it out by the tongue through the mouth.

Hence, it is after the Father, who is the Soul of God, has communicated the exact moment of the second coming of Jesus, who is the Body of God, to Him that He will know. There would be an interval between when the Father would communicate His command of Jesus to come the second time and when He would hear the command. This time interval may be infinitesimally small, but it is there, anyway. There would also be an additional time interval when He (Jesus) would take action to come.

Finally, just before Jesus ascended into heaven, the disciples asked Him a question. In Acts 1:6 they asked, "Lord, will You at this time restore the kingdom to Israel?" His answer sheds light on His second coming. He answered, "It is not for you to know times or seasons which the Father has put in His own power" (Acts 1:7). One of the events in the calendar of God which He has put in His own power is the time or season He will send Jesus to the earth the second time.

It is, indeed, true that without the knowledge of the Trinity of God and how the three Personalities who are One Spirit relate, the deep things of the Bible cannot be well understood.

How to Be Ready

We are to watch out for incontrovertible evidence with regard to His coming. I perceive that the disappearance of people as stated in Matthew 24:40–41 is to be watched out for. The texts say, "Then two *men* will be in the field: one will be taken and the other left. Two *women will* be grinding at the mill: one will be taken and the other left." A pilot and a co-pilot shall be in the cockpit, the one shall be taken, and the other left.

From the different encounters of Jesus with a lawyer and a scribe, we see that through love, the unfeigned type demonstrated by the Samaritan and acknowledgment of Jesus as God, we shall inherit eternal life. These are to be complemented by being busy doing what God ordained one to do. If He meets a minister doing what He commissioned him or her to do, such a minister will qualify to be taken (Matthew 24:45–47). Jesus describes those who are following Him as the salt of the world. It is by having salt in oneself (Mark 9:50) will one be ready for the Second Coming of the Lord Jesus Christ.

The First and Second Ends of the Ages

Apostle Paul in 1 Corinthians 10:11 speaks of two "ends" of the ages. The text says, "Now all these things happened to them as examples, and they were written for our admonition, upon whom the ends of the ages have come. Therefore let him who thinks he stands take heed lest he fall." I shall call the attention of the reader to two things in verses 6 to 10 of the Epistle above.

The first is the list of the things that happened to the Israelites for which they were destroyed. They are five in number.

- They lusted after evil things;
- They became idolaters;
- They committed fornication;
- They tempted Christ; and
- They complained (murmured).

The second is the plural noun "ends" in the phrase "ends of the ages." Two ends of the world are mentioned. The first is mentioned in Hebrews 9:26–28a. It says, "He then would have had to suffer often since the foundation of the world; but now, once at the end of the ages, He has appeared to put away sin by the sacrifice of Himself." So, the first "end of the world" was marked with the offering of Christ to bear the sins of many…." By His voluntary offering, the way to heaven was opened up through His precious blood which He shed for the remission of man's sin. From that point, it became appointed unto men once to die, but after this the judgment.

The second "end of the ages" is referred to in Hebrews 9:28b. It says, "To those who eagerly wait for Him (Jesus) He will appear a second time, apart from sin, for salvation." This is called the rapture. It will happen suddenly. To those who are living and looking for Him, will He suddenly appear in the air to take away within a twinkling of an eye.

Are you ready for this celestial flight? My prayer is that readers of this book will not miss it if they are still alive by the time it takes place.

How To Become Perfect as the Father Is

When Jesus resurrected, Mary Magdalene was the first person He appeared to. When she saw Him, I perceive that she made a move to cling unto Him. But He restrained her, saying, "Do not cling to Me, for I have not yet ascended to My Father…" (John 20:17). He, however, instructed her to go tell His brethren that He was ascending to His Father and their Father, and to His God and their God. He went up to open the way to God the Father with His precious blood.

In John 5:25–26, Jesus said, "Most assuredly, I say to you, the hour is coming, and now is, when the dead will hear the voice of the Son of God; and those who hear will live. For as the Father has life in Himself, so He has granted the Son to have life in Himself, and has given Him authority to execute judgment also, because He is the Son of Man."

So, following His resurrection, He started to exercise the authority that the Father had granted Him. He carried out four assignments in succession. First, He spoke to the souls of the saints of the Old Testament era which had been in paradise, the comfortable part of hell. Second, He resurrected those that heard His voice. Third, He evacuated them to heaven. The record of evacuation can be found in Matthew 27:52–53. They were the people of faith, such as Abel, Noah, Abraham, Isaac, and Jacob who were justified by their sacrifices (Psalm 50:5). Their sacrifices were the means by which they showed that they were looking forward to the sacrifice of Jesus for the remission of sin. From that point on, the soul of any believer in Him that dies goes straight to heaven to await the resurrection of his body from the grave.

Apostle Paul mentioned the word "paradise" in his record of a man in Christ who was caught up to the third heaven. He noted, in particular, that such a man was caught up into paradise (2 Corinthians 12:4). Paul's mention of that word with reference to heaven suggests that Jesus carried out a fourth assignment. He probably moved the entire space called paradise to heaven. I suppose that this is why, according to Isaiah 5:14, "…hell has enlarged itself…." Hell enlarged itself so as to include the space hitherto occupied by paradise.

Jesus also executed judgment on those folks that did not look forward to Him. Consequently their souls continued to suffer torment in hell. The justification and judgment of the saints and sinners respectively, were like preambles to what Jesus will do before His millennial reign commences.

At the end of the age, the full prophecy of Matthew 25:31–46 will take place. Jesus confirmed this future event in John 5:28–29. He will replay it by first raising all who are in the graves. He will then divide them into two groups. There will be the first group of sheep, who are called the righteous (Matthew 25:37). This is the group that did good. Their resurrection will be to life. There will also be the second group of goats, who are called the cursed (Matthew 25:41). This is the group that did evil. Their resurrection will be to condemnation.

The Lord Jesus, in Matthew 5:48, enjoins us to be perfect, even as our Father in heaven is perfect. To be perfect means to become like

God the Father. This, however, will happen only when the bodies of people of faith in the graves shall have been resurrected. With reference to the people of faith, the author of Epistle to the Hebrews says, "And all these, having obtained a good testimony through faith, did not receive the promise, God having provided something better for us, that they should not be perfected apart from us" (Hebrews 11:39–40).

The resurrected bodies of the people of faith would have become immortal (eternal) and incorruptible like that of Jesus. They would also have been merged with their respective souls which had hitherto been in heaven. This is the means to become perfect as the Father in heaven is perfect.

The people of faith whose resurrected bodies have been merged together with their respective souls will, however, not be perfected in isolation. Their combined souls and resurrected bodies will still have to wait for the New Testament saints to be resurrected and also merged with their respective souls. They will then be perfected together.

In Revelation 6:9–11, Apostle John bears witness to this truth. The text says, "When He *(Jesus)* opened the fifth seal, I saw under the altar the souls of those that had been slain for the word of God and the testimony which they held. And they cried with a loud voice, saying, 'How long, O Lord, holy and true, until You judge and avenge our blood on those who dwell on the earth?' Then a white robe was given to each of them; and it was said to them that they should rest a little while longer, until both *the number of* their fellow brethren, who would be killed as they were, was completed."

The people of faith that are living will then experience the rapture after the resurrection of all the dead at the end of the age. Both the resurrected and raptured people of faith will together commence the millennium reign of Christ. The people on earth will also start to suffer severe tribulations.

The resurrected and perfected folks in heaven will then see God the Father, His Son, Jesus Christ, the Spirit, and the host of the holy angels (John 17:21). Such people will greatly enjoy in heaven when they see Jesus of Nazareth. He will usher them into their respective mansions (John 14:2–3).

The resurrected people in hell will also be greatly tormented by Satan and his demons. Such people's torment in hell will be severely painful. This is because they will be seeing Satan and his demons that they had been deceived to serve, when they were on the earth, tormenting them. And to imagine that the punishments will be endless, will make them all the more painful.

I hope that any reader of this book will not neglect the opportunity which belief in Jesus makes possible to become incorruptible and immortal. It is only through Him that anyone can escape from the eternal torment in hell, in the hands of Satan and his cohorts.

CHAPTER 12

Spiritual Process of Conversion

The noun "conversion" was touched upon briefly in Chapter 11. It shall be more exhaustively addressed in this chapter. According to *Oxford Minireference Dictionary*, as a verb, "convert," means "'change from one form or use to another; cause to change an attitude or belief.' As a noun, a 'convert,' means a 'person converted, especially to a religious faith,' hence the noun 'conversion.'"

With the noun, 'conversion,' the element of process is introduced in changing from one stage to another. When conversion is the issue in the Scripture, the spirit will have a part to play. Hence this chapter is entitled, "Spiritual Process of Conversion."

Nicodemus, a religious chieftain of the Jewish sect known as the Pharisees, who was also a ruler, visited Jesus at night. He first said to Jesus, "Rabbi, we know that You are a Teacher come from God; for no one can do these signs that You do unless God is with him" (John 3:2).

Nicodemus came alone. He, however, used the first-person plural pronoun, "We," with reference to those of them who knew that He was a Teacher (Rabbi) from God. It suggests that he was representing a group of people. Jesus might have been a subject of discussion in their meetings. He was thus coming out as a representative of the group – or one who felt concerned about what that group had discussed – to interview Him. Jesus, however, did not bother to ask him who the people he was representing were. He would know who they were, if he was representing some people.

Jesus, immediately, however, took the discussion in a different direction away from focusing on Himself. It was like He did not enjoy Nicodemus praising Him. Greek philosopher Socrates is quoted as saying, "Strong minds discuss ideas, average minds discuss events, *(and)* weak minds discuss people."[11] Nicodemus was a type of the weak minds that discuss people. But, at least, he was bold enough to come out to meet Him, even though it was in the night that he did.

Understanding of Spiritual Process of Conversion

Jesus responded to his comments by introducing two issues. One of them was what would rather make God to be with anybody. For the purpose of clarity, it is not by being a teacher or performer of signs. It is also not by being a ruler in the society or a member of a sect like the Pharisees. It is not even by being religious either. Instead, it is by being *born again* (italics for emphasis) that God will be with anybody.

For a deep understanding of spiritual process of conversion, the word "soul" in a few of the statements of Jesus during this discussion shall be replaced with the word "man." First, Jesus states the fundamental issue thus: "Most assuredly, I say unto you, unless one is born again, he cannot see the kingdom of God" (John 3:3). This is tantamount to saying that it is someone who is born again that could have God be with him.

This fundamental requirement confused Nicodemus. Good enough, he did not hide his ignorance. He, therefore, asked two questions. The first is, "How can a man be born when he is old?" The second is a suggested answer to his first question. It is: "Can he enter a second time into his mother's womb, and be born?" By his two questions, Nicodemus showed that he was, essentially, focusing on biological birth and the physical dimension of human life.

Second, Jesus took Nicodemus away from focusing on this physical dimension of human life to the spiritual. He said, "Most assuredly, I say to you, unless one is born of water and the Spirit, he cannot enter

[11] https://www.goodheads.com > quotes

into the Kingdom of God. That which is born of the flesh is flesh and that which is born of the Spirit is spirit" (John 3:5–6).

Jesus, by His statements, clearly identified two types of birth. The first is physical while the second is spiritual. When a man is, firstly, born of the flesh, it is flesh. That it is flesh means that the decision to give birth to him is that of the parents. It is an operation that hasn't the input of the person that is to be born. The parents only played their token part by mating. God then granted their desire by bringing about his or her conception. Such a person is born into the physical realm. The physical realm is made up of a family and religion which he or she did not have the opportunity to choose. The parents then, at birth, take whatever God gives them.

But when a man is, secondly, born of the Spirit, it is an operation that has the input of the person that is to be born. Such a person is born into a family that he chooses. But the Scripture says that a man can receive nothing, unless it has been given to him from heaven (John 3:27; 19:11).

So, like the conception and birth in the flesh by the earthly parents are given from heaven, being born again of the Spirit is also given from heaven. For the sake of distinction, the latter is called "born again." It means that the man who is born again chose to "believe also in Jesus." He has thus been converted to a new man by the Spirit of God. The man is then born into the spiritual realm from the physical. A man cannot receive anything unless it is given to him from heaven (John 3:27). Therefore, heaven is also in charge of a man being born of the Spirit of God.

Does it then mean that a man that is not born again is not given the grace to be so born from heaven? The answer of the Scripture to this important question introduces the issue of belief which this book centers on. The relevant Scripture is Mark 11:24. It says, "Therefore I say to you, whatever things you ask (desire) when you pray, believe that you receive *them,* and you will have *them.*"

Whosoever, therefore, desires to be born again, and prays to the Father in heaven through Jesus Christ, he or she is automatically born again. The person should immediately believe that he or she has been born again of the Spirit of God. This is despite the fact that he or she does not experience any physical change in his body. As a matter of fact, the hosts of heaven are already celebrating over such a person (Luke 15:7). The converted person should immediately start to confess with the mouth about the reality of what has taken place in the spiritual realm. By confessing with the mouth, the newly born again person is activating his or her faith. This is why Hebrews 11:6 says that without faith it is impossible to please God.

The Story of Peter

Let me, additionally, shed some light on the import of the phrase "spiritual process of conversion" by citing some examples. The first addition is through the story of Peter.

Peter was a fisherman when Jesus called him to follow Him. He promised to make him a fisher of men. The text Mark 1:16–18 says, "And as He walked by the Sea of Galilee, He saw Simon and Andrew his brother, casting a net into the sea; for they were fishermen. Then Jesus said to them, 'Follow Me, and I will make you fishers of men. They immediately left their nets, and followed Him.'" The verb "left" means that they literally walked away from their means of livelihood, which was fishing.

At a point in their course of following Jesus, Satan desired to sift Simon Peter as wheat. This was when he began to trust in his might and power to help his Master in the spiritual battle which was ahead of Him. He failed to realize that the battle before Him shall neither be fought by might, nor by power, but by the Spirit of the Lord of hosts

(Zechariah 4:6). At this point, Jesus raised an alarm. He said to him, "Simon, Simon! Indeed, Satan has asked for you, that he may sift you as wheat. But I have prayed for you, that your faith should not fail; and when you have returned to *Me,* strengthen your brethren" (Luke 22:31–32). The instruction of Jesus to Peter means that when you become converted or spiritual, rather than carnal, strengthen your brethren.

Peter had been following Jesus for about three and a half years, but he had not yet been converted by the Spirit of God. Peter's conversion, however, did not come easy. This was despite that he was to soon graduate from his discipleship program and had also initially left or forsaken his fishing occupation. He needed to make an irrevocable decision to follow Jesus. This decision is, first, carried out through the mouth and heart. Paul describes this process thus: "That if you confess with your mouth the Lord Jesus and believe in your heart that God has raised Him from the dead, you will be saved" (Romans 10:9). It is after taking these initial steps that the Lord would seal his or her decision by baptizing him or her with the Holy Spirit.

> **Whosoever, therefore, desires to be born again, and prays to the Father in heaven through Jesus Christ, he or she is automatically born again.**

With respect to Peter, within the space of forty days after His resurrection, Jesus appeared to the disciples at various times and places. The third time that He would appear to seven of them was at the Sea of Galilee. Peter had led six other disciples back to fishing. These were some of his brethren whom his Master had instructed him to strengthen when he is converted. They fished all night but caught nothing. It was a fruitless work. By morning, Jesus appeared to them. Initially, they did not know that it was He. He asked them if they have any meat. Their answer was, "No!" He then instructed them to cast the net on the right side of their ship, and they would find. They obeyed and caught a multitude of fish.

Finally, Jesus fed them on fish and bread which He supplied! He gave them fresh fish by their sudden catch and ready-fried fish, and bread to eat. He then squarely faced Peter. Peter, whom the Father had chosen as the potential leader of the group by revealing who Jesus is to, seemed to be the main focus of His visit. First time, He asked him, "Simon, *son* of Jonah, do you love Me more than these?" He was most probably pointing a finger at the fish in the net while asking him the question. Peter answered, "Yes, Lord; You know that I love You." Jesus said unto him, "Feed My lamb."

The second time, He asked him, "Simon, *son* of Jonah, do you love Me?" He answered the same way as before; and the Lord said unto him, "Tend My sheep."

The third time, He again asked him if he loved Him. It was as if He drove a sharp needle into Peter's thick skin by asking him the third time if he loved Him. It was the same number of times he denied his Master during His trial. He answered, "Lord, You know all things; You know that I love You." Jesus again said unto him, "Feed My sheep." Jesus instructed him to feed His lamb once, and sheep two times (John 21:15–17). He finally instructed him to follow Him.

Two times did Jesus instruct him to follow Him (John 21:19, 22). He obeyed. He did by first expressing his love for the Lord. He then confirmed his obedience by making up his mind to fully follow Him. This was when he actually believed that Jesus is alive and is worth following. Jesus, thereafter, baptized him and the other disciples with the Holy Spirit on the Day of Pentecost in Jerusalem. Peter was thus converted by the Spirit of God. He then permanently walked away from his fishing business by which he was making money. He totally and finally forsook it and changed over to another "fishing business". By his spiritual conversion, Peter started to harvest people into the

Kingdom of God. Jesus assured him that he would glorify God with his death in his old age (John 21:18–19).

That Peter fully followed Jesus does not imply that God disapproves of part-time ministerial work. My definition of a part-time minister is that the person is both a spiritual and physical worker. Apostle Paul as a part-time spiritual worker was enabled by the Spirit to bear the fruit of the Spirit. He was also able to perform miracles, and win souls into the Kingdom of God. And as a physical worker, he was a tent maker. His hands ministered unto his physical necessities and of those that were with him, and of the weak that he also supported (Acts 18:3; 20:34–35).

God Partnered Judaism with Christianity through Jesus

Peter, eventually, permanently walked away from his fishing business, and was sealed with the Holy Spirit. That was when he added "belief in Jesus" to his earlier "belief in God." It had been proved that Judaism is the equivalent of "belief in God." By virtue of Jesus being the epitome of the everlasting Kingship of Judah from whose name Judaism is derived, He is thus the King of the Jews. The wise men from the east attested to this. When Jesus was born in Bethlehem in Judea, they came looking for Him whom they called the King of the Jews. They had seen His star in the sky and had come to worship Him and to give Him presents (Matthew 2:1–12). And by virtue of the role He played in the establishment of Judaism in the wilderness on Mount Sinai, He is the Head of Judaism.

Jesus was also involved with the establishment of the Church. This important spiritual move which took place in the Upper Room on the Day of Pentecost in Jerusalem has been touched upon in Chapter 9. That day He started to build His Church as per His promise in Matthew 16:18. The text says, inter alia, "…I will build My church, and the gates of Hades shall not prevail against it."

The adherents of the Church were later called Christians in Antioch by those who identified them as followers of Christ (Acts 11:26). The religion was later called Christianity. Christianity is thus the equivalent of "belief in Jesus," and Jesus is also its Head. In summary, Jesus was the head of the Church, His body, in the wilderness, in the Old Testament, as well as the head of His Church, in the New Testament.

If the head of a man is separated from the rest of his body, the result will be the death of the man, head and body. In like manner, if Jesus, the Head of the Church, is separated from the Church, the body of Jesus (Ephesians 5:23, 30), the result should be instant death of the two. But Jesus had been from everlasting to the point when He was made a flesh (John 1:14).

At the age of about thirty three and a half years, He was crucified for the sin of mankind. But on the third day, He was resurrected. He, thus, conquered death. He could, therefore, no more die after His resurrection. Consequently, He would continue to live from everlasting to everlasting. He has thus gotten eternal life which He is ready to bequeath to any member of His Church.

In the Old Testament, Judaism is called "the Church in the wilderness" (Acts 7:38). Its adherents consisted mostly of the Israelites. Other nationals with them were the mixed multitude that came out from Egypt with them (Exodus 12:38). In the New Testament the initial members of the Church of Jesus were His disciples who were also mostly Israelites (Jews). Following the acceptance of other nationals who had repented of their sins and had received the gift of the Holy Spirit, the membership of the Church became enlarged.

Following the persecution of the young Church by the leadership of the Jews, the adherents scattered abroad. However, they continued to preach Jesus wherever they went. Signs and wonders also happened in their ministry. The result was that the number of believers further increased. An epicenter of this new move of God was Antioch.

By this time, Paul had been converted from religion, Judaism, to Jesus. Barnabas looked for him and brought him to Antioch. Together, for one year, they taught the people. Those who watched the relationship among the adherents saw that they behaved like Jesus Christ. They, therefore, called them Christians–those who are like Christ (Acts 11:26). The name "Christianity" became the religion of those who are like Christ. This means that those who are not like Christ are not Christians even though their religion may be called Christianity. So, because both Judaism and Christianity make up the Church, the Head of which is Jesus, God thus partnered them together through Him.

The plan of God concerning the adherents of both religions is well articulated by Apostle Paul. In a nutshell, he says, "And that He might reconcile them both (adherents of Judaism and Christianity) to God in one body through the cross, thereby putting to death the enmity …. For through Him we both have access by one Spirit to the Father" (Ephesians 2:16–18). It would appear as if Satan was privy to this plan. He, therefore, did not waste time in throwing a big spanner into the budding union of the two. The attack was, basically, through circumcision.

Disagreement over the issue of circumcision resulted in disaffection between the adherents of the two religions. Judaism emphasized circumcision of the flesh as necessary for acceptance (Genesis 17:9–13). Apostle Paul, however, regarded circumcision of the heart, which comes through spiritual conversion, as sufficient (Deuteronomy 10:16; 30:6; Jeremiah 4:4; Romans 2:29).

The result was a parting of ways. A sustained antagonism against the Jews by some "European Christians" heightened the irreconcilable differences. But, it is to the glory of God that the two sides are now being brought close together so as to achieve the plan of God. The organization called *Christians United for Israel* (CUFI) is an arrowhead of this move.

Worship and Work

Going by the role that Jesus played, two things will hold sway concerning someone who experiences spiritual conversion. One, the new convert will worship God in spirit and truth through Jesus. Two, the new convert will complement his worship of God with good works which can be done through religion (Judaism or Christianity).

Hence Apostle James could define religion as visiting the fatherless and widows in their affliction, *and* to keep oneself unspotted from the world (James 1:26–27). And in our present dispensation, it includes providing food, water, shelter, and medicines for millions of refugees. These are made up of people displaced by war, famine, climate change, natural disaster, and environmental pollution.

The text of Apostle James above contains a few of the good works that Jesus listed in Matthew 25:31–46. Jesus would classify people either as sheep or goats on the Day of Judgment on the basis of the works they did while on earth. The sheep will be those that did good works, while the goats will be those that did evil. But does the classification as sheep imply that a man can gain entry into the kingdom by his good works?

The Scripture says, "For by grace you have been saved through faith, and that not of yourselves: *it is* the gift of God, not of works, lest anyone should boast" (Ephesians 2:8–9). This Scripture shows that the classification of some as sheep does not imply that anyone can gain entry into the kingdom by his good works. It, however, means that the goats with their evil works do not have an iota of chance to enter into the kingdom.

One must, first and foremost, be saved by grace through faith. And it is the prerogative of Jesus to save man, for He is the Savior. Anyone that is so saved is described as "the righteous" (Matthew 25:37). But the one that is not so saved is described as "the cursed" (Matthew 25:41). Jesus is thus the only Savior of the world and not any religions, including Judaism and Christianity or the multitudes of other religions which could be embodiments of good works.

Some adherents of Judaism and Christianity might read this assertion and condemn its abiding thesis. They are entitled to their views. But Jesus would tell such people that He knew them not at the point of asking Him to open the door into the kingdom for them. They would even claim that they performed miracles in His name. Yet He would turn them back as workers of iniquity who did not enter by the narrow gate (Luke 13:24–30).

As for the Jews, Jesus also asserts that people from the east and west would sit with Abraham, Isaac, and Jacob in the kingdom. Unfortunately, the children of the kingdom will be locked out (Matthew 8:10–12; Luke 13:22–30). Apostle Paul summarizes what Prophet Isaiah prophesied hundreds of years earlier in Isaiah 10:22–23. He says, "Though the number of the children of Israel be as the sand of the sea, the remnant will be saved…" (Romans 9:27).

Satan, the Devil, is the prince of this world (John 12:31). A man whose spirit has been renewed by the Spirit of God continues to dwell in the world. Therefore, Satan, the prince of this world, can still try to manipulate him through his flesh which is weak. The spirit of such a man and his flesh are, thus, constantly in conflict. While the Spirit of God will try to guide him into all truth through his spirit, Satan will also try to lure him to do evil works through his flesh. Such evil works include adultery, fornications, uncleanness, lasciviousness, idolatry, witchcraft, hatred, variance, emulations, wrath, strife, seditions, heresies, envyings, murder, drunkenness, and revellings. Those who do such works cannot inherit the kingdom of God (Galatians 5:19–21).

Salvation of Man from Sins

The second addition to "spiritual process of conversion" is derived from the message of God through angel Gabriel to Joseph. Matthew

1:21 says, "And she *(the Virgin Mary)* will bring forth a Son, and you *(Joseph)* shall call His name JESUS, for He will save His people from their sins." Judaism with its laws, commandments, rituals, and good deeds was expected by a Jew to save him. But here is God saying, loud and clear, that they are not able to save a man or soul from sin. So JESUS came to do what religion could not do.

Walking after the Spirit

The third addition to the "spiritual process of conversion" is derived from the long address by Apostle Paul to the brethren in the text of Romans 7:1–8:5.

I shall not bother to reproduce the long text. It, however, highlights the role of the Spirit of God in the process of spiritual conversion through believing in Jesus as the Savior from sins. The new convert then starts to walk after the Spirit.

Though the flesh is still very active in the new man, a drastic step must be taken to put it in check. Paul used the phrase "put to death." This is a drastic measure to put it in check. Otherwise, it can kill the new man. He says it thus: "For if you live according to the flesh, you shall die; but if by the Spirit you put to death the deeds of the body, you will live" (Romans 8:13). This is what it means to be walking after the Spirit.

This thought, however, was not original with Paul. It was the Lord Jesus who said earlier that if any part of a man's body will lead him into hell, it were better for him to cut it off. This is because it is better to go to heaven without a particular part of the body than to go to hell with every part of it (Matthew 5:29; 18:9; Mark 9:47).

An unsaved person, as a soul, will be subjected to torment in hell beneath the earth (Matthew 10:28). The story of the rich man in Luke 16:19–31, which is referred to earlier, confirms this outcome. A saved person, as a soul, is carried into heaven where he lives in comfort. The translations of Enoch and Elijah into heaven are good examples to point to (Genesis 5:24; 2 Kings 2:11). They were not translated as flesh and blood (1 Corinthians 15:50), but as flesh and bones. Jesus was carried into heaven as flesh and bones (Luke 24:39). Every believer in Jesus will also be carried up as flesh and bones. This is because God would have made him/her the righteousness of God in Jesus and not in religion.

PART V

Saul Became Born Again

This part consists of two chapters. Both are devoted to the experience of Apostle Paul. The first is his experience entirely in Judaism. It is presented hypothetically. The second is His practical experience in Christianity.

CHAPTER 13

The Initial Objective of Paul

Paul's Hypothetical Mission Statement

Saul of Tarsus, who became Apostle Paul, provides us with a classic example of someone who initially got stuck in the religion of his fathers, Judaism. He was determined not only to live by the tenets of that religion but to also ensure that whoever veered away from it was stoutly resisted or punished. He did not mind wasting the lives of people whom he considered to be giving their allegiance to "another God." He did not know that he was "sincerely wrong." He did not know that without Him (Jesus), the religion that he was defending is empty. He did not know that He is the Son of God and that His disciples were the ones he was persecuting. But he eventually enjoyed the grace of God and became born again.

Paul's hypothetical mission statement shall be presented. It shows what his activities in the course of pursuing his goal of eliminating the adherents of *THE WAY* could have been. The activities were intended to benefit Judaism, the religion of the Old Testament era, of which he was then a member.

The Objective of Saul of Tarsus

The objective of Saul of Tarsus in his self-imposed assignment can be stated thus: "I, Saul, whose name means great, am determined to be the best among my peers in my zeal for God's work. This is because the zeal of God's house has eaten me up; and the reproaches of them that are reproaching Him by calling one "impostor," the Christ, the Son of the Living God, are fallen upon me (Psalm 69:9).

"I shall, therefore, embrace the strictest sect of the Pharisees. To become one of the best in the Law of Moses, I shall enroll in one of the best Law Schools in the nation, especially that of Gamaliel, a renowned lawyer. With my legal accomplishment, I can become zealous in the defense of the Law of Moses. I shall, thereby, be able to fight the cause of the God of my fathers."

Guidance by the Law of Moses

"I, Saul, shall be guided by the Law of Moses. If I were not circumcised on the eighth day, I would have presented myself in my adult age for circumcision because of my confidence in the flesh. After all, our father Abraham was circumcised at the age of 99 and I am not as old as he was. I trust totally in the flesh. Therefore, I shall personally persecute, from synagogue to synagogue, the members of the Church of Jesus. These are a group of people who do not trust in the Law of Moses. Instead, their allegiance is toward the so-called grace and faith of one Jesus of Nazareth, who is also called the Son of God."

Avoidance of Marital Hindrance

"I shall endeavor to avoid any forms of marital hindrances. This decision is meant to prevent the important family life that can hinder me from carrying out my chosen assignment against the Church. I shall, therefore, be able to freely move from place to place and, at any time I choose. This will enable me to carry out my assignments flawlessly."

Easy Access to Religious Leaders

"I shall ensure that I have easy access to the religious leaders of my nation. This will afford me the opportunity to take active part in any event that involves the persecution of the followers of the 'so-called Jesus of Nazareth.'" [Saul eventually kept the clothes of those that stoned Stephen until he died (Acts 7:58; 22:20).]

Learning Law and the Scripture

"I shall also try hard to be knowledgeable in the Scripture. Both qualifications will enhance my self-esteem. After all, I am of the stock of Israel, of the tribe of Benjamin. I am of the royal stock, the tribe that produced the first king of Israel, King Saul, the son of Kish. My parents must have taken cognizance of this history; hence I am named 'Saul' after the name of that first king of Israel. I am, thus, a Hebrew of Hebrews – a complete Hebrew."

Sources of Strength and Joy

"I shall continue to derive strength and satisfaction from the leadership of my nation by persecuting the Church of Jesus. I shall also derive joy from seeing the people of the so-called Son of God hauled into prison. And this I shall pursue to any length and place, both inside and outside the nation of Israel."

The Benefit of the Zeal of Saul

The benefit of the zeal of Saul was that it afforded him the opportunity to have the ears of the leadership of Judaism, the religion of the Jews. They were made up of the high priests, the Pharisees of which he was a member, and those that matter in society. He was thus able to carry out a lot of havoc against the Church of Jesus without suffering any sanction from the government of the day. But he did not know that there was a supreme God above that was carefully monitoring his steps.

It is the same God who is overseeing the affairs of all that are happening in the whole world even now. He will not fail to impose His sanction at His appointed time.

CHAPTER 14

The Final Objective of Paul

Paul's Final Mission Statement

Saul, who was later popularly called Paul, had set out on his journey from Jerusalem with letters from the high priest to the synagogues in Damascus. His self-imposed assignment was to arrest either men or women of the Way (Church) and bring them bound to Jerusalem. This was another step he took to expand the frontiers of his persecution of the Church. He took steps within and without the territory of Israel. This was after the active part he played in the killing of Deacon Stephen, the first Christian martyr. He kept the clothes of those who stoned him until he died (Acts 7:58).

Jesus, the owner of the Church, who had been given all power in heaven, on earth, and under the earth, confronted him on the way to Damascus. As has been documented in Scripture, it was Jesus that won the battle. He used His word and light, not bow and arrows, to attack and subdue Saul in that encounter.

When Saul was knocked down on his way to Damascus, he heard a voice saying, "Saul, Saul, why are you persecuting Me?" There was no mistaking the fact that the person calling his name knew him pretty well. Saul asked, "Who are You, Lord?"

It is note-worthy that Saul recognized the person who had knocked him to the ground as Lord even though He had not yet mentioned His name. He asked him why he is persecuting Him. To have called the unknown person, "Lord", showed that Saul believed in God. This was why he was doing the entire things that he did in an apparent support of Him.

So, like Jesus acknowledged that His disciples believed in God, so He had also acknowledged that Saul believed in God. Saul only needed to be moved to a relationship with Him, hence He appeared to him. He came to redirect him. In doing so, there would be two advantages to derive. One would be for Saul. He would be put on the path to fulfilling his destiny. Two, he would become useful to the Kingdom of God.

To have called the unknown person, "Lord," showed that Saul believed in God. This was why he was doing the entire things that he did in an apparent support of Him.

The Lord answered his question, saying, "I am Jesus, whom you are persecuting." By this time, Saul had fallen to the ground. It was a hard knockdown that the Lord had given him. Saul instantly recognized Him and then sought to know what He would have him do. The Lord dictated his mission statement to him. He instantly accepted Him as Lord and was converted. He instantly abandoned the religion that he had been persecuting the disciples of Jesus for. He eventually entered Damascus being led by hand having been blinded by a brighter light than that of the sun which he saw. He was lodged in the house of one Judas in Straight Street.

Saul was redirected. He was "sincerely wrong" in all that he was doing against the Church because of ignorance which he later acknowledged. He said, "And I thank Christ Jesus our Lord who has enabled me, because He counted me faithful, putting *me* into the ministry, although I was formally a blasphemer, a persecutor, and an insolent man; but I obtained mercy because I did *it* ignorantly in unbelief" (1 Timothy 1:12–13). God found him doing what he was doing with all his heart and diligently too. He was applying the measure of faith that God dealt to him (Romans 12:3) with all his heart. God then reordered him in exercise of His grace and mercy.

Paul Lived Before in the Religion of the Old Testament Era

Several statements are credited to Paul that the life he lived before he encountered Jesus was being in the religion of the Old Testament era – Judaism. He once had opportunity to defend himself before King Agrippa. He had been accused by the Jews of activities that were contrary to the Jewish religion. He said in his defense, "My manner of life from my youth, which was spent from the beginning among my own nation at Jerusalem, all the Jews know. They knew me from the first, if they were willing to testify, that according to the strictest sect of our religion I lived a Pharisee" (Acts 26:4–5).

He also testified to the Galatians, saying, "But I make known to you, brethren, that the gospel which was preached by me is not according to man. For I neither received it from man, nor was I taught *it,* but *it came* through the revelation of Jesus Christ. For you have heard of my former conduct in Judaism, how I persecuted the Church of God beyond measure and *tried to destroy* it. And I advanced in Judaism beyond many of my contemporaries in my own nation, being more exceedingly zealous for the traditions of my fathers. But when it pleased God, who separated me from my mother's womb, and called me through His grace, to reveal His Son in me, that I might preach Him among the Gentiles, I did not immediately confer with flesh and blood" (Galatians 1:11–16).

The life that Paul lived before in religion could not have taken him to the Father, his zeal notwithstanding. The grace he received motivated his decision to alter his objective.

I Shall Be Guided by the Grace of Jesus

"I shall, henceforth, be guided by the grace of Jesus. Whatever the Lord would have me to do, I am ready (Acts 9:6). As a minister and witness for the Lord, I shall handle my assignments with more zeal than I demonstrated for my former inglorious work. I shall not be disobedient to the heavenly vision. I shall commence immediately to witness of the resurrection of the Lord that gave me life more abundantly. I shall go to Jerusalem and Judea and to the uttermost parts of the earth (Acts 1:8) as the Lord mandated His disciples to preach the gospel of the Lord that I once persecuted. My message shall be none other than, 'Repent and turn to God and do the works meet for repentance.'"

I Shall Remain Unmarried

"In my new dispensation, I shall continue to regard marriage as one of the hindrances to ministry. Therefore, I shall remain unmarried, and also not reap carnal things such as money from adherents, so as not to hinder the gospel of Christ" (see 1 Corinthians 9:5 and 11-15).

I Shall Not Compromise the Gospel

"The other disciples and other Church members shall be my family members. My relationship with them shall be cordial. But whenever and wherever the Gospel would be compromised, I shall always take a position for the truth of the Gospel." [He did oppose Peter on the matter of circumcision (Galatians 2:11–14).]

"I shall be ready always, even to the point of death, to suffer for the Gospel. Therefore, anybody that cannot suffer for the Gospel cannot be my companion." [He cut off with John Mark. He, however, reconnected with him showing that Paul was ready to forget the past and move on.]

The Holy Spirit Shall Be My Strength

"I shall rely on the Holy Spirit to be the supplier of the strength and safety that I need to do my ministry. Therefore, I shall give quality time to prayer (Acts 9:11). I shall equally seek supplication from other brethren. No number of threats to my life will make me to refrain from preaching the Gospel. I shall preach to both small and great."

I Shall Strive to Understand the Scripture

"The Scripture shall be a major pillar of strength for me. Therefore, I shall strive to understand it. I shall then profusely deploy it. I shall stick to the old time message, saying none other things than those which the prophets and Moses did say should come."

I Shall Preach the Gospel Systematically

The main content of my message shall remain as:
1] "That Christ should suffer;
2] "That Christ should die;
3] "That Christ should be the first that should rise from the dead;
4] "That Christ should show light unto the Jews; and,
5] "That Christ should show light unto the other nations."

My Message Shall Be Detailed

"I shall always affirm what Jesus did or did not do when He was on earth. For example, whatever He did was not in secret. I shall strive to be detailed and convincing in the presentation of the message." [King Agrippa said that Paul almost persuaded him to be a Christian. Festus could not help describing him as a man with much learning which had made him mad (Acts 26:24).]

He was determined to always wish every hearer of the word be converted like him but without the chains on his hands.

I Shall Continue to Learn

Paul went to Arabia for about three years, locked himself up and learned the Scripture from the point of view of the new light which he had received on his way to Damascus. He requested that his books and parchments be brought to him (2 Timothy 4:13). He could then read more. It is interesting that he made this request when he was at the end of his ministry. In effect, it was death that literally stopped him from continuing to learn through reading.

I Shall Communicate the Gospel Effectively

He was also determined to strive to communicate the gospel effectively. He would thereby shed light on the sayings of the Lord as the Spirit of God would enable him. [Peter even acknowledged that some of his writings are rather difficult to understand.]

Conclusion of Paul's Ministry

Paul concluded his ministry on a note of accomplishment as he declared: "I have fought the good fight, I have finished the race, I have kept the faith" (2 Timothy 4:7). More startling a declaration of Paul was the one which he made to the Ephesians at Miletus. He said as a parting statement, "Therefore I testify to you this day that I *am* innocent of the blood of all men" (Acts 20:26). He was able to make such a declaration through strict implementation of his mission statement.

Where do you think that Apostle Paul is now? He is in heaven, of course, for he fought the good fight. He finished the race. He kept the faith. He is wearing the crown of righteousness which the Lord Jesus gave him (2 Timothy 4:7–8). This is what the Father has prepared for all those who choose to believe in God and believe also in Him.

The true story of Saul of Tarsus strongly advises that no one should get stuck in religion by believing in God alone. Instead, everyone should rather enter into a new relationship with Jesus as Paul did by being genuinely converted.

The true story of Saul of Tarsus strongly advises that no one should get stuck in religion by believing in God alone. Instead, everyone should rather enter into a new relationship with Jesus as Paul did by being genuinely converted from religion to Jesus. Those that do will happily accompany this great Apostle in the Kingdom of God.

PART VI

Final Appeal

This part has only one chapter. It is a plea to every reader to do what the book recommends.

CHAPTER 15

Don't Believe in God only, Believe in Jesus also

Jesus Clearly Stated His Assignment

Jesus had introduced Himself to those who were looking out for Him after He fed them with bread as, "The bread of life." Jesus said that anyone who comes to Him shall never hunger, and he who believes in Him shall never thirst (John 6:35). He then stated that they had come to Him, they had seen Him, but they had not believed in Him. He then took time off to explain to the people what His assignment was.

He says, "All that the Father gives Me will come to Me; and the one who comes to Me I will by no means cast out. For I have come down from heaven, not to do My own will, but the will of Him who sent Me. This is the will of the Father who sent Me, that of all that He has given Me I should lose nothing, but should raise it up again at the last day. And this is the will of Him who sent Me, that everyone who sees the Son and believes in Him may have everlasting life; and I will raise him up at the last day" (John 6:37–40).

Dear reader, you will remember that earlier in Chapter 8, it's said that the Father has committed all judgment unto the Son. The Father did this so that everyone should honor the Son, just as he honors the Father. By using the word "all" as an adjective to qualify "judgment" in the sentence above, Jesus indicated that at that future date, the totality of the works of the Father would be handed over to the Son. Unfortunately, they were not prepared to abide by the will of the Father to recognize and honor Him as God. It certainly became too late for those fellows.

Why God Needs to Draw a Person to Himself

In John 6:44, Jesus says, "No one can come to Me unless the Father who sent Me draws him; and I will raise him up at the last day." He equally says in Matthew 11:28, "Come to Me, all *you* who labor and are heavy laden, and I will give you rest." Does His statement in the first scripture put the blame for those that fail to come to Him on apparent refusal of the Father to draw them to Him?

Jesus first explained how a man can come unto Him. He says, "It is written in the prophets, 'And they shall all be taught by God. Therefore everyone who has heard and learned from the Father comes to Me'" (John 6:45). The second statement of Jesus in Matthew 11:28 is an example of what to hear and learn about the love of God. It is an appeal to everybody who is laboring and is heavily laden to recognize that God has provided rest with Jesus for such people ready for the taking.

It would be expected that anyone who is laboring and heavily laden, after hearing and learning about the love of God for mankind (John 3:16), would readily come over unto Jesus so as to enjoy the rest that He promises. But it does not happen that easily. Jesus said that it is still necessary for the Father to draw such a person to Jesus.

If a man can receive nothing unless it is given to him from heaven, it also means that no man can receive salvation or rest from Jesus unless God first draws such a person to Him.

Jesus simplified this requirement for us to understand with a reference to the role of the Father. He said, "Therefore I have said to you that no one can come to Me unless it has been granted to him by My Father" (John 6:65). This simplified requirement, notwithstanding, we still need to know the fundamental reason why it is essential that God needs to draw a person before he can come to Jesus.

Jesus is also involved with drawing people to Himself because He is also known as the everlasting Father (Isaiah 9:6). This is because Jesus is "the Body of God," while God the Father is "the Soul of God." And as the body of man covers and carries the soul of man, so did Jesus cover and carry God. Whoever, therefore, has seen Jesus has also somehow seen the unseen God who is on the inside of Him [Adeoye].[12]

Jesus also does what God the Father does. Jesus describes His form of drawing thus: "And I, if I am lifted up from the earth, will draw all *peoples* to Myself" (John 12:32). It is, therefore, the sinless life that He lived, His crucifixion for the sins of mankind, and resurrection by God that qualified Him to be able to draw many to Himself. This is also a confirmation that He is one with the Father (John 10:30).

Jesus is the "Body of God," while God the Father is the "Soul of God." And as the body of man covers and carries the soul of man, so did Jesus cover and carry God.

Force of Religion and Custom

At birth, everyone becomes stuck in one form of religion and custom or the other. The society everyone is born into also exercises some measure of stiff control over its new arrivals or citizens. The stiff control can even be done through initiation which, after it is subscribed to, one must not violate without suffering a dire consequence. It is the same attitude that the parents of the new arrivals [into their midst by birth] invariably also tend to put up. The society dictates what to do and what not to. It is even worse that this controlling influence seems to persist after one attains the age of accountability which is generally put at eighteen years.

The use of the word "draw" means the call or summons by either of the Father or Son. Force is applied so as to overcome the strong pull of religion and any other custom. The pull tends to prevent the people

[12] Adeoye, Adedeji David: *Op cit:* It provides more of this exposé in its pages.

from willingly choosing to come to Jesus Christ. The restraining pull of religion can be so strong that it will require the stronger force of God the Father or Jesus to free one from its grip. Do not get stuck to religion at the initial stage of belief in God. Do not let it tie you down. It must let you convert to Jesus.

Do not get stuck to religion at the initial stage of belief in God. Do not let it tie you down. It must let you convert to Jesus.

This issue can be illustrated with what happens between an airplane and the force of gravity that tends to prevent it from flying. The airplane is designed to fly in the air. That is its operational zone. But its engine power has to overcome the force of gravity that is acting to prevent it from flying. It is after this that it can go up into the sky to do what it is designed and manufactured to do best. This is how the forces of God the Father and of the Son need to exceed the strong force of religion and custom. Both religion and custom seem to work together to hold down everybody that is created and formed or born from coming to Jesus.

The airplane attains its potential by flying in the sky after overcoming the force of gravity. In like manner, man will attain his potential by changing over to Jesus Christ. This is what happens after converting from one's religion to Jesus.

From the initial universal level on which everyone expresses one's belief in God, He expects everyone to move up and embrace Jesus as the Savior. By Him, everyone can find fulfillment of one's destiny. Each person will be able to find the way back to God the Father at the end of one's sojourn on earth. This was a privilege that a person like Paul enjoyed.

The simple definition of destiny is reaching one's destination. And the destination of everybody that comes to the world is God the Father. His throne is in heaven. It is called the Kingdom of God. Jesus said,

"I came forth from the Father and have come into the world. Again, I leave the world and go to the Father" (John 16:5, 28). This is how it should be for everybody. And because Jesus had successfully opened up the way to the Father (Hebrews 9:26), everybody can then get to the Father through Him. It is by believing also in Him that anyone can enjoy this opportunity. It is not by getting hooked on religion at the stage of belief in God. Therefore, don't get lost on the way from earth to heaven. Do not be distracted by religion. Let the Spirit of God lead you home.

Man will attain his potential by changing over to Jesus Christ. This is what happens after converting from one's religion to Jesus.

How God Draws a Person to Himself

The ways God/Jesus draws a person include, but not limited to, the following:

1. God, first of all, gives each person a measure of faith (Romans 12:3).
2. God will raise an intercessor for such a person.
3. God will use someone to invite the person to the Lord and be saved. In the alternative, Jesus can decide to appear to someone as He did to Paul.
4. God will raise someone to visit and counsel the person.
5. God will teach the person through a teacher of the word of God.
6. God can decide to do some specific miracle as a sign to demonstrate His compassion for such a person.

The Times of Ignorance

The example of Apostle Paul confirms the involvement of both God the Father and the Lord Jesus. God the Father and Jesus drew Paul by a force greater than any religion has.

With Paul's (Saul's) experiences in both "belief in God," and "belief also in Jesus" by which a person can become a new creature, with old things past away (2 Corinthians 5:17), he qualifies to define the former state as "the times of ignorance." Time in the religion of the fathers, to borrow Paul's term (Acts 24:14), is a time in ignorance (Acts 17:30). God is always ready to forgivingly wink at such a time. This is provided that such people would obey His commandment. There is no preference for any color, nationality, custom and tradition. All that is needed is conversion to Jesus. This is because He had appointed a day in which He will judge the world in righteousness by *that* Jesus. He had shown Him to all by resurrecting Him from the dead {Acts 17:30–31}.

I Will Raise Him up

There are two ways that the verb, "raised" is used in connection with Jesus. The first is as used by Jesus Himself. With this verb, He meant to bring back certain people from the dead. The second is as used by the disciples of Jesus with regard to Him. By it, they meant that the Father raised Jesus after His crucifixion. Jesus will raise four categories of people.

The first category is the person whom the Father had given Him. Jesus says it this way, "This is the will of the Father who sent Me, that of all He has given Me I should lose nothing, but should raise it up again at the last day" (John 6:39). His disciples fall into this category. During His speech cum prayer in Chapter 17 of John's Gospel, which are directed at the Father, Jesus said, "I have manifested Your name to the men whom You have given Me out of the world. They were Yours, You gave them to Me, and they have kept Your word" (John 17:6).

The second category is the group of persons that will see the Son. He states it thus, "And this is the will of Him who sent Me, that everyone who sees the Son and believes in Him may have everlasting life; and I will raise him up at the last day" (John 6:40). The emphasis here is on the verb "see". This condition concerned those who lived when He was in the world. Those of them that saw Him and believed in Him to be the Son of God would be raised up. This condition further suggests that Jesus wished everybody that lived at the time He came to the world to be His disciples. He did not restrict the membership of His disciples to only the Twelve He called and ordained to follow Him. This way, Jesus manifested His impartial nature.

This view can be verified by the statements He made at one forum. Jesus healed someone who was sick of palsy. He saw the faith of the four people who conveyed the sick folk to the venue. He saw their faith through what they did. They removed the whole roof over the venue where He was holding the meeting and dropped the man with the palsy in front of Him. He then said to the sick man, "Son, your sins are forgiven you" (Mark 2:5). The scribes at the venue took offense. They said in their hearts, "Why does this *Man* speak blasphemies like this? Who can forgive sins but God alone?"

Jesus immediately perceived in His Spirit that they so reasoned within themselves. He then said unto them, "Why do you reason about these things in your hearts? Which is easier, to say to the paralytic, '*Your* sins be forgiven you,' or to say, 'Arise, take up your bed and walk?' But that you may know that the Son of Man has power on earth to forgive sins"–He said to the sick of the paralytic, "I say to you, arise, take up your bed, and go to your house'" (Mark 2:8–11).

Jesus chose to address the issue of the sin of the sick man so that the others around may choose to take advantage of His power to forgive sins and ask for the forgiveness of theirs. This is more so because, "For all have sinned and fall short of the glory of God" (Romans 3:23). And of course, that was His main reason for coming to the world. Instead, they focused on finding fault with His words.

Record also has it that Jesus had more than twelve disciples. There was a time He appointed other seventy also, and sent them two by two before His face into every city and place where He Himself was about to go (Luke 10:1). Apostle Paul says that He was seen of above five hundred at once after His resurrection (1 Corinthians 15:6).

The third category of persons is also defined by Jesus. It is, "Whoever eats My flesh and drinks My blood has eternal life, and I will raise him up at the last day" (John 6:54). These are the people that ate the bread and drank the wine of the New Covenant in His body and blood (Luke 22:19–20). Such persons must have come to Him when they were alive. In short, they must have been born again.

The fourth category of persons is equally defined by Jesus. He declares during His lengthy prayer before confronting Golgotha, "I do not pray for these alone, but also for those who will believe in Me through their word; that they all may be one, as You, Father, *art* in Me, and I in You; that they also may be one in Us, that the world may believe that You have sent Me.... Father, I desire that they also whom You gave Me may be with Me where I am, that they may behold My glory which You have given Me; for You loved Me before the foundation of the world" (John 17:20–21, 24).

Jesus would have had to raise people that had died before such people could be with Him where He would be. On the other hand, such people would have had to be raptured. Such people would not only behold His glory, they would also share in it.

The Promised Prophet

Following the filling of the disciples with the Holy Spirit on the Day of Pentecost, Apostle Peter preached to the mammoth crowd. In his reference to Jesus being raised up, he quoted what Moses said, saying, "For Moses truly said to the fathers, 'The LORD your God will raise up for you a Prophet like me from your brethren. Him you shall hear in all things, whatever He says to you'" (Acts 3:22).

Apostle Peter identified the promised Prophet as Jesus of Nazareth. He said, "To you first, God, having raised up His Son Jesus, sent Him to bless you, in turning away every one *of you from his iniquities*" (Acts 3:26). The Father resurrected Him from the dead on the third day after

His crucifixion. What God the Father did for Him, He will in turn do, on the last day, for those that had believed in Him when they were on earth. He will raise them up.

They will then be with Him where He is, that they may behold His glory (John 17:24). They will not only behold His glory, they will also appear with Him in glory (Colossians 3:4). This means that the glory of God by which a believer in Him had been short of (Romans 3:23) would have been added.

Let not any reader of this book miss this opportunity.

PART VII

Appreciation by Jesus

This last part has only one chapter. It presents what rewards whoever "believes in God" and "believes also in Jesus" will receive at the end of his or her life on earth.

CHAPTER 16

Jesus Will Say, "Thank You"

A Servant that Does Not Deserve "Thank You"

A story of a faithful servant is recorded in Luke 17:7–9. Jesus used it to show who does not deserve "thank you." He says,

"And which of you, having a servant plowing or tending sheep, will say to him when he has come in from the field, 'Come at once and sit down to eat'?

"But will he not rather say to him, 'Prepare something for my supper, and gird yourself and serve me till I have eaten and drunk, and afterward you will eat and drink'? Does he thank that servant because he did the things that were commanded him? I think not."

Jesus addressed this story to the masters in that society. It implies that if such masters will not say, "Thank you", to their servants, they should not expect God, the overall Master, to say thank you to them for doing their duties to Him.

Jesus concludes the story of the "faithful servant" in Luke 17:10 thus, "So likewise you, when you have done all those things which you are commanded, say, 'We are unprofitable servants. We have done what was our duty to do.'"

As stated earlier, Peter changed his business from fishing to make money to become fishers of men. By the new business, he was harvesting people into the Kingdom of God. Those who do the latter business are adjudged by God to be wise (Proverbs 11:30). And because they are wise, they shall shine as the brightness of the firmament. And as they continue to turn many to righteousness, they shall shine as stars for ever and ever (Daniel 12:3). But those that love the former (money), have erred from the faith, and pierced themselves through with many sorrows (1 Timothy 6:10).

Daniel who received this revelation was instructed by God to shut up the words, and seal the book, *even* to the time of the end; many shall run to and fro, and knowledge shall increase (Daniel 12:4). This is the appointed time. Technological advancement which has turned the world into a global village with the preponderance of internet facilities confirms the truth of the Bible. And I am very grateful that it pleased the LORD God to choose even me to be involved with this truth. The end is, indeed, very near.

Jesus Will Confess Him or Her as His

Jesus says, "Therefore whoever confesses Me before men, him I will also confess before My Father who is in heaven. But whoever denies Me before men, him will I also deny before My Father who is in heaven" (Matthew 10:32–33). Those that confess Jesus before men are those that decided to add belief in Jesus to their earlier belief in God. Literally, they converted from their religion to Him, while still maintaining their belief in God. Jesus will say "Thank you," to such people by confessing them before the Father in heaven. This group of people would be raised up to live eternally with Him. This means a replacement of their temporal life with eternal. What a big way to say, "Thank you!"

On the contrary, those that deny Him before men are those that refuse to accept Jesus as the Savior. Jesus will not say, "Thank you", to such persons. This will be by denying them before the Father and His holy angels.

Jesus Will not Be Ashamed of Him

Jesus again says, "Therefore whoever is ashamed of Me and of My words in this adulterous and sinful generation, of him the Son of Man also will be ashamed when He comes in the glory of His Father with the holy angels" (Mark 8:38; Luke 9:26). The contrary is also obvious.

Whoever will not be ashamed of Jesus and of His words, of him shall He not be ashamed at the end.

There is the common saying that, "Show me your friend, and I will tell what type of a person you are." The Scripture complements this common saying thus, "Do not be deceived: 'Evil communications corrupt good habits'" (1 Corinthians 15:33). Jesus would not like His good manners to be corrupted. He would thus state unequivocally, "… I tell you I do not know you, where you are from. Depart from Me, all you workers of iniquity" (Luke 13:27).

Jesus and a Malefactor

Jesus was nailed to the cross at Golgotha, the place of a skull. Two malefactors were also nailed to their individual crosses, one on the right side of Jesus and the other on His left. The rulers and the soldiers mocked Him. The rulers, in particular, mocked Him, saying, "He saved others; let Him save Himself, if He is the Christ, the chosen of God." Jesus did not respond to their mocking.

One of the two criminals also railed at Him. He was imitating the mockers. He said, "If You are the Christ, save Yourself and us" (Luke 23:39). This criminal openly declared his rejection of Jesus being the Son of God. He thus rejected the only provision of God by which everyone can escape from perishing (John 3:16).

But the other, answering, rebuked him, saying, "Do you not even fear God, seeing you are under the same condemnation? And we indeed justly, for we receive the due reward of our deeds; but this Man has done nothing wrong. Then he said to Jesus, Lord, remember me when You come into Your kingdom" (Luke 23:40–42).

Jesus literally thanked this other malefactor for his confession of Him with thirteen eternal words. They are, "Assuredly, I say to you, today you will be with Me in paradise" (Luke 23:43).

My Father Will Honor Him

Jesus Christ said, "If any man serve Me, let him follow Me; and where I am, there My servant will be also. If anyone serves Me, him *My* Father will honor" (John 12:26). You can believe in a God whom you do not see. But you cannot follow a God whom you do not see. And because we need to see the person we are to serve and follow, hence, God sent Jesus, His only begotten Son, to us.

He told His disciples to "follow Him and He will make them fishers of men." Whoever is serving and following Him, is doing so to God who is invisible (John 1:18; 5:37; Colossians 1:15; 1 Timothy 1:17) for they are one (John 10:30). He (God) will honor anybody that does.

Even though Jesus cannot be seen physically now, records about Him are there to learn from. Any interested person can read and endeavor to practise what He did. Such a person is following Him vide His teaching. This is what informs His instruction to His disciples to go and teach all nations to observe all things whatsoever He has commanded them (Matthew 28:19–20).

There is no honor that is greater than this. It is the singular way to escape from hell, which is the name of the eternal abode for those that got hooked in religion.

The Father will Honor Them

Those that heed His command to go teach all the nations accordingly, Jesus would heal them. This is a way of saying, "Thank you," to them. There is no honor that is greater than this. It is the singular way to escape from hell, which is the name of the eternal abode for those that got hooked in religion.

Afterword

I shall conclude this narrative with two points on how Jesus opened the way for man to the presence of God. The first is by believing in Him to be the Son of God and understanding the Scripture. The second is by blending His ministerial mission with the everlasting feasts of God.

I. Believe Jesus and Understand the Scripture

God gave Jesus to the world as an expression of His love for it. But the enjoyment of this love by anybody is conditional. The person must believe that Jesus is the Son of God. Paul told the jailor of the prison in which he and Silas were kept in Philippi, "Believe on the Lord Jesus Christ, and you will be saved, you and your household" (Acts 16:31). Before one could believe the Lord Jesus Christ, however, one must hear the Scripture, the word of the Kingdom of God.

We learn from the Parable of the Sower, which is recorded in Matthew 13:3–4, that the seed that fell by the wayside did not bear fruit because the birds of the air devoured it. Jesus interpreted the birds as the wicked one, Satan, the Devil (Matthew 13:18–19). He, Satan, quickly comes to catch away the word from the heart of any man that does not understand it. Therefore, one must not only hear the word, one must also understand it. By understanding it, the word is thus sown in one's heart. The wicked one is not able to snatch the word sown in the heart of a hearer that understands it. The word will then be able to do what God intends it to do for such a person.

God gave Jesus to the world as an expression of His love for it. But the enjoyment of this love by anybody is conditional. The person must believe that Jesus is the Son of God.

So, believing in Jesus and understanding the word of God would prevent someone from perishing. God showed His love for mankind by putting forward belief in Jesus, while pushing backward understanding of the Scripture. This is because Satan can easily tamper with the word in the heart or mind of a man, especially if he does not understand it. But he cannot easily tamper with what he believes. And it is when someone has believed in Jesus as the Son of God that he can start to understand the Word of the Kingdom of God. It is rather unfortunate, however, that several people do not toe the easier path, the path of *belief* (italics for emphasis) in Jesus. Instead they are toeing the path of *understanding* (italics for emphasis) the Scripture, the Word of the Kingdom of God. This is very convenient for the arch enemy. He can thus easily lead such people astray. This is why through lack of understanding of the Scripture one finds a teaching like this: "God did not give birth to a Son." Such a teaching shows that such people do not know the difference between "the Seed of God" and "the seed of man."

Burnt, sin, peace, trespass, and meat offerings had been dispensed with by the singular offering and sacrifice of Jesus on the cross at Calvary, but not the feasts.

Such people also do not believe Hebrews 13:8. The text says, "Jesus Christ is the same yesterday, today, and forever." So, while rejecting this eternal attribute of Jesus, they readily claim that they believe in Him. They even acknowledge His supernatural conception, and that He performed miracles. They go off track, however, by teaching that Jesus was relevant only in the past when He appeared physically on earth. Such people teach that Jesus is no more relevant now and in the future. Such people are not true believers in Him. Their assumption is a big lie concocted by Satan, the Devil, to lure multitudes of people into hell.

II. Jesus Recognized the Everlasting Feasts of God

Jesus recognized and observed the everlasting feasts of God. A few of them are the feast of Passover and unleavened bread, the feast of Pentecost (Weeks), and the feast of Tabernacles (Booths) (Deuteronomy 16:16). For example, He became our Passover Lamb (1 Corinthians 5:7). It was also in the middle of the feast of Tabernacles that He made an announcement about the living water. He invited anybody that is thirsty to come and take the water and drink (John 7:37–39).

Jesus celebrated His last feast of Passover in the Upper Room in Jerusalem. It was the same day that He inaugurated the New Testament in His body and blood. Judas Iscariot took part in them. He did so in sin and rebellion and went to perdition as a result. Satan, his sponsor, who had the power of death was also thereby stripped of his power of death (Hebrews 2:14). On the other hand, Jesus who loved the world including Judas Iscariot and addressed him as "friend" was delivered from death by resurrection. Paul could, therefore, warn that everybody that comes to the table of the Lord to eat and drink must examine himself, if there is ought that he should repent of, and then eat, and drink (1 Corinthians 11:28).

Jesus recommended the Passover feast, which is now called Holy Communion, to be observed continually in remembrance of Him. He said further that as often as His disciples do it, they do show His death until He comes. I dare say that anybody can celebrate this feast yearly, monthly, weekly, or daily. Whoever makes it to heaven will partake in the feast of Passover and Unleavened Bread. This was the assurance Jesus gave to His disciples at the concluding moment of the inauguration of New Testament in His body and blood. He said, "With *fervent* desire I have desired to eat this Passover with you before I suffer; for I say unto you, I will no longer eat of it until it is fulfilled in the Kingdom of God" (Luke 22:15–16).

Burnt, sin, peace, trespass, and meat offerings had been dispensed with. This was because of the singular offering and sacrifice of Jesus on the cross at Calvary. The feasts, however, were not dispensed with. Hebrews 10:5–14 attests to this. Israel was to keep it by an ordinance forever (Exodus 12:14, 24). Every genuine convert to Jesus will celebrate it with Him in the Kingdom of God.

Congratulations

For reading *God without Jesus: The Making of Empty Religion* to this point, I say congratulations. Can you say that you have been blessed by its content? If your answer is "Yes", please, give the praise to God who brought it your way and do not fail to do what it demands of you.

There is life after life. God brought this book your way so that you may abide with Him in His Kingdom of Comfort at the end of your life here on earth. You should not fail to add "belief in Jesus" to your "belief in God". It is their combination that can take anybody to that Kingdom of Comfort. Do so, and you will not regret your decision forever. Failure to do so foretells danger of eternal damnation. Please, make a good choice. Cheers.

Bibliography

The New King James' Version (NKJV) of The Holy Bible.

The Authorized King James' Version (KJV) of The Holy Bible.

Abraham, Ayomide: *Daily Showers… January 2020 edition* (Published by Ayomide Abraham, 3, Adebayo Drive, Temidire, Sango, Ota, Ogun State, Nigeria.

Adeoye, Adedeji David: *Jesus and the Trinity: What Many Believers Don't Know* [Page Turner Press and Media, Chula Vista, California (2019)

Google.com @www.theregister.co.uk/

https://www.personalexcellence.co>blog on https://www.google.com

https://www.google.com

Huch, Larry: *4 Blood Moons: Your Future Begins Now,* [Published by Winters Publishing, LLC 2448 E. 81st St. Suite #4802, Tulsa Oklahoma 74137 USA, (2014).]

Matthew Henry: *Concise Commentary On the Whole Bible* [published by Operation Mobilization Literature, Waynesboro, Georgia, by arrangement with Moody Press c/o MLM, Chicago, Illinois, USA, (1995).]

Shakespeare, William: *Julius Caesar* [https://www.britannica.com>topic>Julius….]

CPSIA information can be obtained
at www.ICGtesting.com
Printed in the USA
LVHW040530200122
708837LV00002B/58

9 781638 718604